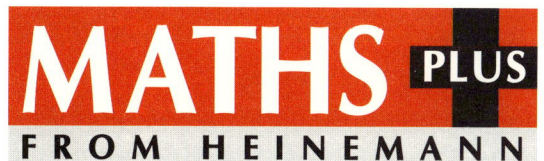

MATHS PLUS
FROM HEINEMANN

Nursery Mathematics

writing team

Anne Desforges ● Val McGrath ● Janet Morris
Linda Mort ● Carole Skinner

editorial team

Patti Barber ● Sue Gifford
Penny Munn

Heinemann

Heinemann Educational Publishers
Halley Court, Jordan Hill, Oxford OX2 8EJ
a division of Reed Educational & Professional Publishing Ltd

OXFORD MELBOURNE AUCKLAND
FLORENCE PRAGUE MADRID ATHENS
SINGAPORE TOKYO SAO PAULO
CHICAGO PORTSMOUTH NH (USA) MEXICO CITY
KAMPALA NAIROBI KUALA LUMPUR

First published 1997

99 98
10 9 8 7 6 5 4 3 2 1

ISBN 0 435 02373 X

Designed and typeset by Gecko Limited, Bicester, Oxon
Cover design by Gecko Limited, Bicester, Oxon
Printed and bound in Great Britain by George Over Ltd.

Commissioned photography by Trevor Clifford

We are grateful to the children and teachers at
Deepdale Infant School, Preston, and
Faringdon Infant School, Faringdon for their support in
producing the photographs for this book.

The publishers would like to thank Ladybird and
Orchard Books for their permission to use the books
photographed on page 68, and Jonathan Langley for the
illustrations within Jonathan Langley's Nursery Treasury
(publisher: Harper Collins).

Contents

Introduction

Nursery Mathematics is written for people who work with young children. It contains ideas for activities that have the potential for rich and varied mathematical experience, to give children a good start in their mathematical education.

The activities are based on three principles of how young children learn:
- from experiences in which they feel secure and confident – both at home and at school
- with people who are interested in them, and what they are doing, and who know the learning potential of the situation
- by talking and thinking about their experiences

The activities also reflect the fact that children come to nursery with different levels of experience, interest and expertise. The belief is that all children can learn mathematics provided that we observe what they can do and provide appropriate experiences which can develop their mathematical interest.

Using the activities within a happy and unpressured environment will ensure that children's mathematical expertise will develop towards (and, where appropriate, beyond) the SCAA *'Desirable Outcomes for Children's Learning'* and Scottish *Pre-school Education Initiative*. This approach is consistent with the SCAA 'Common features of good practice', as it combines comfortable challenges and sensitive intervention, with ongoing observation and assessment, and also involves parents as partners.

How the book is organised

Nursery Mathematics is arranged in three maths content-focused sections:

    Number
    Measures
    Shape and Space.

A fourth section, 'Routines and Special events', allows you to choose an activity to fit in with nursery routines in a more incidental way. Activities in this section are set within an overall theme and contain aspects of number, measures, and shape and space.

Using the activities

The activities have been designed to be used with children who are at a range of developmental stages. They can therefore be used in any order. For each activity the following presentation has been used:

Description of the activity, setting the context and indicating its potential.

The main mathematical focus for each activity, to aid planning.

Example questions and mathematical language you might use to develop the maths aims.

Sample responses to help gauge what the children understand and do, and the kind of strategies and language they are using. The responses are highlighted to link with the appropriate item on the development grid. (See page 6.)

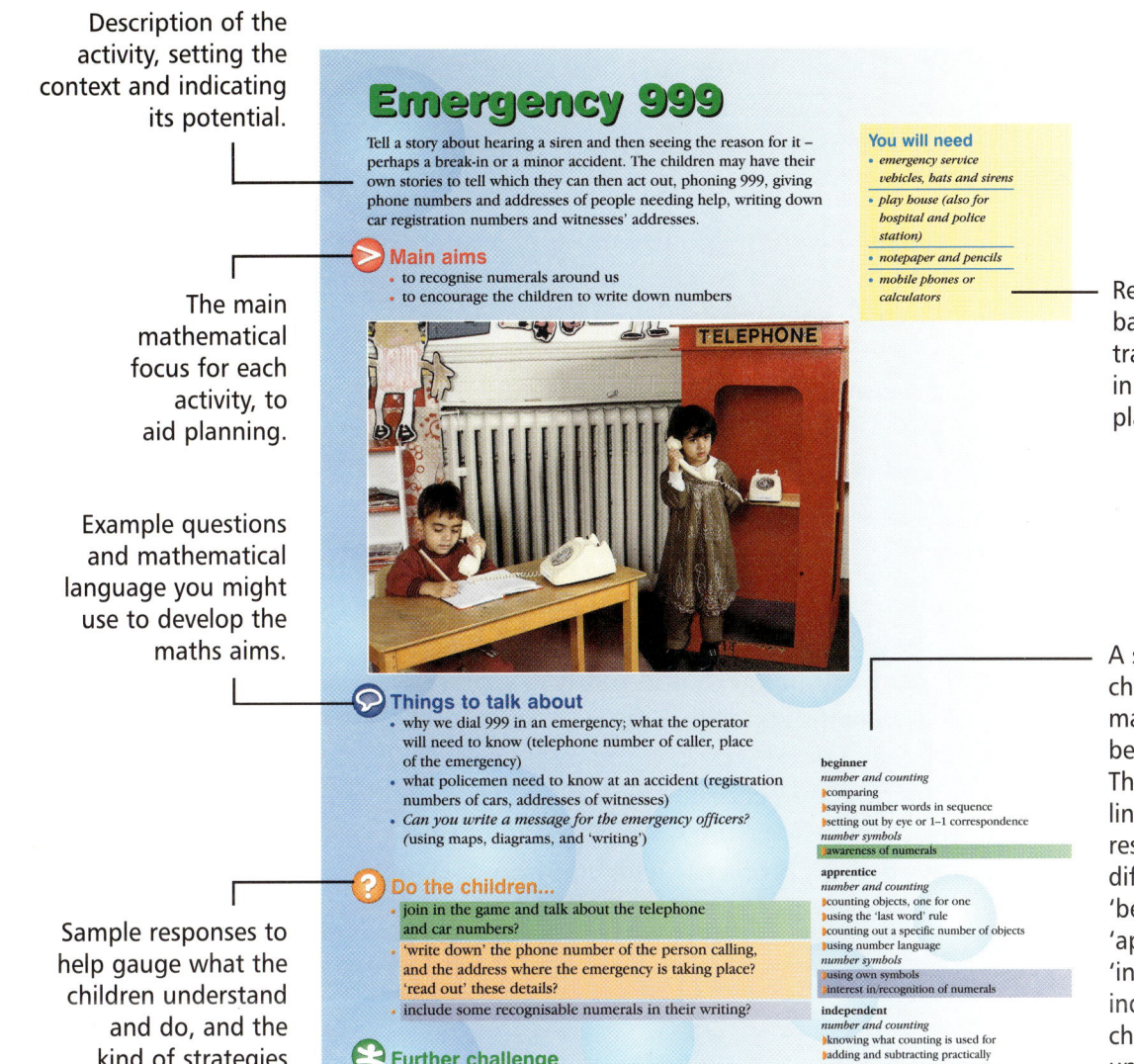

Emergency 999

Tell a story about hearing a siren and then seeing the reason for it – perhaps a break-in or a minor accident. The children may have their own stories to tell which they can then act out, phoning 999, giving phone numbers and addresses of people needing help, writing down car registration numbers and witnesses' addresses.

You will need
- *emergency service vehicles, hats and sirens*
- *play house (also for hospital and police station)*
- *notepaper and pencils*
- *mobile phones or calculators*

> Main aims
- to recognise numerals around us
- to encourage the children to write down numbers

◯ Things to talk about
- why we dial 999 in an emergency; what the operator will need to know (telephone number of caller, place of the emergency)
- what policemen need to know at an accident (registration numbers of cars, addresses of witnesses)
- *Can you write a message for the emergency officers?* *(using maps, diagrams, and 'writing')*

? Do the children...
- join in the game and talk about the telephone and car numbers?
- 'write down' the phone number of the person calling, and the address where the emergency is taking place? 'read out' these details?
- include some recognisable numerals in their writing?

🌱 Further challenge
- Children can describe the route to their home.

22

beginner
number and counting
- comparing
- saying number words in sequence
- setting out by eye or 1–1 correspondence
number symbols
- awareness of numerals

apprentice
number and counting
- counting objects, one for one
- using the 'last word' rule
- counting out a specific number of objects
- using number language
number symbols
- using own symbols
- interest in/recognition of numerals

independent
number and counting
- knowing what counting is used for
- adding and subtracting practically
- solving number problems mentally
number symbols
- matching numerals with amounts
- writing numerals
- reading and writing for a purpose

Resources required, based on equipment traditionally found in nurseries and playgroups.

A summary of how children's mathematical behaviour develops. The highlighting links the children's responses to different levels: 'beginner', 'apprentice' and 'independent'. This indicates how the children's understanding might develop next, in breadth as well as progression. (See page 6.)

Suggestions for developing the activity or the area of mathematics. Other possibilities will occur to you and the children, such as letting children decide what numbers to use in a game.

A progression for how children learn mathematics

In all aspects of mathematics, but particularly in number, we suggest that there are three stages of development: beginner, apprentice and independent. These reflect the child's developing social awareness, and have implications for the role of the adult – which changes at each stage.

At the *beginner* level, children are aware of some mathematical aspects of experience, such as the position of things in relation to themselves. They use informal language such as 'a lot' and 'a little' and may know some number words. The appropriate adult role is to provide experiences for the child to explore, and to use mathematical language to describe those experiences.

At the *apprentice* level, children are beginning to use more precise mathematical language for themselves, such as 'tall', 'more than' and 'next to'. The adult role is to provide social experiences where mathematical language is part of the activity, such as action rhymes, cooking or tidying up. As adults and older children provide models of how mathematics is used, children may role play 'measuring' or use 'counting-like behaviour' but without full understanding. For example, they may count a group of objects but not know how many they have counted.

At the *independent* level, children can use mathematical tools for a purpose. For instance, they may spontaneously count to solve a problem of putting out enough plates, read a numeral to find out how many pens should be in a pot, or consult a drawing to make a model. This is quite sophisticated behaviour, which may not be shown by many four year old children. Particularly with measuring, nursery age children are very unlikely to use units, independently, to measure with. The role of the adult at this level is to pose and discuss problems with children, encouraging predictions and explanations, and trying out strategies.

The development grids

Children do not learn different aspects of mathematics in a clearcut, linear sequence. With counting, for instance, children may simultaneously be learning to say the numbers up to 20, when they are only making sets of up to ten, and recognising numerals up to 5. However, *Nursery Mathematics* provides an idealised sequence, based on grouping developmental points within the 'beginner-apprentice-independent' stages, described above, into development grids for Number, Measures and Shape and Space. (See introductions for Number, Measures and Shape on pages 15, 71 and 95 for a full description of these.)

If children are confident in one aspect, you will not necessarily expect them to immediately progress to the next item on the grid in a linear way, as each may take months to develop. Instead, you may plan to develop the same aspect in other activities, or to broaden their confidence and expertise, by focusing on another aspect.

Mathematical content

The development grids (pages 16, 71 and 95) are based on current research into how children learn mathematics. In the past our expectations of young children have sometimes been limited, based on ideas of what mathematics children should learn first, not on what they are ready for. For instance, it used to be thought that children should sort and match before counting, whereas now it is accepted that children learn to count by counting, not by doing pre-counting activities. In *Nursery Mathematics* you will therefore find that there is less emphasis on some familiar activities, such as sorting by colour, whereas others, such as practical problem solving, receive more emphasis.

Mathematical processes, such as communicating, predicting and pattern spotting, as well as areas such as sorting and data-handling, are also included.

Talking with children

Mathematics is about logical systems of number, measurement or classification of shape which have been developed by adults. Children cannot discover these systems by themselves and therefore have to learn a lot of mathematics from other people. *Nursery Mathematics* therefore focuses on how an adult might develop mathematical learning through discussion with the children, by providing experiences and posing problems which are rich in mathematical possibilities. Observing and listening then allows you to pick up on the children's interest and intentions, and to help them to use appropriate mathematical language.

Using a variety of contexts

Young children can learn through a variety of experiences, as long as these are relevant or interesting to them. For instance, they often have an interest in big numbers which, if encouraged, later develops into mathematical understanding. This interest and positive attitude is the key to children learning to be confident mathematicians, and is therefore the first thing to look for in children's mathematical development.

In *Nursery Mathematics* the activities have been included to cover six contexts that are typically part of nursery activity:
- Imaginative play – the home corner, café, hairdressers, garage or travel agents
- Small world – play people, farm, dinosaurs, train sets, roadways, waterways
- Creative – art, graphics, technology, cooking, music
- Structured apparatus and games – building blocks, number rods, shapes, board and card games
- Outdoors – large apparatus, large motor skill activity, gardening, minibeasts
- Group time – stories, rhymes, songs

Planning, assessing and recording

Planning

There are two key considerations when planning nursery activities:
- ensuring a balanced curriculum which incorporates number, measures, shape and space
- reflecting children's interests

The planning for each term should take account of the need for balance. The structure of *Nursery Mathematics,* with separate sections for Number, Measures and Shape, and the focused aims for individual activities, are intended to make it easier to choose an activity, which supports this level of planning.

Activities can then be selected to reflect children's interests, and aid the planning of a balance of different learning contexts on a day-to-day basis. The contents pages for each section (pages 14, 70 and 94) help you to plan activities to enable all children to gain the varied experience they need. We have included a suggestion for a weekly planning format. (See page 10.) This could be used to note key activities within any of the learning contexts included in this book. Another possibility is to use the chart on page 9, which allows you to plan activities to link into ongoing topic work.

Planning opportunities for children to see maths as an integral part of their everyday environment is also important. To this end, a summary of ideas for creating a mathematically rich environment is provided on page 11.

Assessment and recording

By engaging with any of the activities in this book observational assessment can take place as a matter of course. For each activity, the child's response can be interpreted by looking at the link with the development grid. Children do not learn in a linear way and their behaviour will vary from session to session. However, you may occasionally wish to make a note of a child's performance. The observation record on page 12 allows you to record significant achievements, noting the date and the context for the observation.

Parental involvement

Children often do very different things at home from what they do at school. You can often be surprised, when talking to parents, to discover the range of a child's experience. It is therefore important to talk to parents and encourage their involvement. Suggestions for questions to ask parents about what their children can do, together with a series of photocopiable activities to be used at home, are provided from pages 150–159.

Topic-planning grid

Theme/Maths topic	Ourselves	Calculators and IT	Mini-beasts/animals	Patterns	Toys and games	Homes/buildings	Vehicles	Food and farming	People who work for you
Number and counting	Fun in the park	Calculator fun	Noah's ark Collecting bears Bear races Teddies in tunnels	Repeating patterns Decorated plate line Musical codes Crocodile	Hiders and seekers Box numbers Jump to it! Pass the parcel Put in five Sand buckets Beanbag throw Route march Copy cat Find a friend On the move Who's next?	Hiders and seekers Model street Castles	Blast off! All aboard! Car parks Trains	Don't break the eggs! Penny shop One for you, one for me Decorated biscuits Hungry robot Food times	Glove puppet magic show
Number symbols	Number books Birthday card shop Personal numbers	Calculator calls		Musical codes	The hopping line Beanbag throw Route march On the move Under the blanket	Table for 3?	Trains Boat loads	The supermarket Cooking numbers Librarians	Emergency 999 Box office A letter for me
Measures	Baby's bath water Shoe shop Beds for bears At the hospital Stretching	Forwards and backwards		Tapping toes	Heavy bear	Wallpapering		Dinner in the home corner Filling milk bottles Weighing bags Fruit and vegetable stall The bird table	
Shape and Space	Gift boxes	Roaming robot	Curvy worms Elephant lift Shape snake Block caterpillar	Bandage Elastic stretch Potato roll Dishcloth design Ribbon plait Symmetrical patterns Button up	Russian dolls Find the shape Find the treasure Fill the shape Washing line Kite flying Hide and seek Step hop	Building towers Outside edge Wall hanging Building from plans Making a den	Bike and trike park		

Weekly planner

Week beginning:		Imaginative play	Small world	Creative	Structured apparatus and games	Outdoors	Group time
Monday	am						
	pm						
Tuesday	am						
	pm						
Wednesday	am						
	pm						
Thursday	am						
	pm						
Friday	am						
	pm						

10

Creating a mathematically rich environment

Small children are naturally inquisitive and if their environment is rich in written numbers and math-related resources then it is easy for adults and children to initiate talk about maths concepts. For instance, if the home corner has familiar appliances with numbers on, then children can relate their home experiences of number to the nursery environment. If adults refer regularly to numbers on clocks, calendars, registers and measures, then children can begin to appreciate the different purposes and meanings of numbers.

on the ground: carpet tile numbers, hopscotch patterns, number tracks

on the wall: calendars, register charts, number notices, birthday charts, height charts, number friezes

on the shelves: number puzzles, wooden numerals, sandpaper numerals, plastic numerals

on technological appliances: calculators, computers, robots, tape recorders, clocks (watches, alarm clocks, digital clocks, timers), shop till, number clickers, pricing machines, thermometers, scales, home corner appliances (telephone, washing machine, fridge, microwave, radio, TV, VCR)

in books: catalogues, phone books, telephone number index, appointment books, diaries, recipes, registers, page numbers

on reference material: number lines, number friezes, number charts, number books, magnetic numbers

out and about: house numbers, bus numbers, car numbers, street signs, shop signs, tickets, till receipts

How regular is the child's access to such number materials?
Do they notice the numbers, talk about them and play with them?
Are numbers available to handle and refer to in
all areas, inside and out?
Are number charts at child eye level and hand level?
How often do they refer to numbers in charts, books and
calendars, or discuss what numbers on appliances are for?
How often do they notice and discuss numbers
when they are out and about?

Observation record

Name _____

	NUMBER	Observations *(including dates and contexts)*
beginner	saying number words in sequence	
apprentice	counting out a specific number of objects from a larger group	
	using verbal number patterns	
	using own symbols	
	recognising numerals	
independent	knowing what counting is used for	
	solving number problems	
	reading and writing numerals for a purpose	

	MEASURES	
beginner	showing an interest in measures	
apprentice	using the language of measures	
	using direct comparison and ordering	
	engaging with measurement and tools	

	SHAPE AND SPACE	
beginner	showing an interest in shape, position and pattern	
apprentice	using the language of shape and position	
	copying and describing patterns	
	making spatial representations	
independent	making patterns with rules	

Number

Number

Imaginative play

Small world

Creative

Construction and games

Outdoors

Group Time

Number

ADULT *Can you count?*

EMMA *Yes.*

ADULT *Could you show me how you count?*

EMMA *One, two, three, four, five...*

ADULT *Tell me, what do you count in the nursery?*

EMMA *(puzzled) But counting's just saying words, isn't it?*

As adults we share a common view about how number and counting work. It is therefore sometimes difficult to remember that children can have a different view, attaching quite different meanings to the same words. For some children, counting can be 'just saying the words' – a purely verbal activity, unconnected to any objects being counted. Other children may understand that counting is associated with objects and be capable of counting up to 20, 30 or more, co-ordinating the number words with pointing. However, they may not understand that 'how many' refers to the total amount. At this stage it is also rare for children to understand why we count. The reason lies in the way young children learn about number.

When thinking about how young children learn about number it is interesting to look at the parallel development in literacy. Young children learn about reading through adults sharing books and writing with them; we take it for granted that children need daily experiences of books, stories and roleplaying reading to develop literacy. Children learn about number in the same way – by joining in with activities, copying other children, trying out adult activities in pretend play and having conversations about number. From the earliest age, children can use number – even toddlers know about number words, respond to them and use them in conversation. As with literacy, adult conversation plays a crucial role in supporting children's understanding.

The way children use number can be described in terms of the three stages outlined in the Introduction (page 6) and detailed in the chart overleaf.

Number and counting	Number symbols	Adult role
beginner		
• Comparing (using words like _more, a lot_) • Saying number words in sequence • Setting out a specific number of things by eye or by one-to-one correspondence	• Awareness of symbols	• Provide opportunities to join in and copy
apprentice		
• Counting objects, one for one • Using the 'last word rule' to say how many • Counting a specific number of objects (e.g. 'Give me 5' • Using number language – ordinal (first, second, third) – number word patterns	• Using own symbols • Interest in and recognition of numerals	• Provide group structure, e.g. set up games where the children need to count • Demonstrating adult purposes for the number system
independent		
• Knowing what counting is used for • Adding and subtracting practically • Solving number problems mentally (hidden number, spotting number patterns)	• Matching numerals to amounts • Writing numerals • Reading and writing numerals for a purpose	• Discuss goals and purposes • Encourage prediction and explanation • Discuss problems and solutions

Beginner stage

Number and counting

Children at this stage can **compare** amounts, and use this to talk about 'a lot' or 'a little'. They may know several number words (not always in the right sequence) but they don't connect them with amounts by counting.

Before children can count they can recognise small quantities (up to about three or four) by eye. They also learn very early on that we use number words for quantities. So, for example, they can grab a handful of 'three' or 'four' of something. They won't be very accurate for numbers above three or four because they are judging by eye. They can also use one-to-one correspondence or matching to put out the same number of things.

Number symbols

Children using number at this level may be aware of some symbols, but they often don't distinguish between 'letters' and 'numbers'.

How an adult can help

Children are best helped by activities where they can join in and copy others without needing to know the rules. (See, for example, _Sand buckets_, page 53 and _Blast off!_, page 20.) Adults can encourage children to use number by giving plenty of opportunity to copy other children's counting or to work with the very small numbers they can judge by eye. Warmth in relationships is vitally important at this level of function – the more a child likes a person (child or adult) the more the child will copy that person.

Since children learn the counting words ahead of the quantities it is helpful to encourage children to say number sequences at an early age and to talk with them about big numbers. Learning the number words and the counting sequence is the start of learning about the number system.

Apprentice stage

Number and counting

At this level, children are becoming quite fluent at the number sequence and are beginning to **count objects** by saying one number for each object. Some can do this with large numbers but do not yet use the '**last number rule**' to say how many.

ADULT (indicating large pile of 60 bricks) *Can you count these blocks for me?*

JOHN *One, two, three, four, five,...fifty-eight, fifty-nine, sixty.*

ADULT *So how many are there?*

JOHN (deep sigh) *One, two, three, four, five, ...*

Many children at this stage, like John, interpret 'how many?' as a cue to start counting – even for the second time! Other children may not count as far, but are beginning to use this rule. They will sometimes check what they have counted using their rule knowledge to correct any mistakes. When asked to, they will **set out a specific number of things by counting**. Even if they don't count out loud, you will see the count in the hand movement as they carefully put the objects one by one into your hand or their own: they are 'counters' rather than 'grabbers'.

As children become experienced in reciting the number sequence they remember more and more of it. When they get past 'twenty' they start to figure out the rules for generating number words, so they rely more on the rule than on their memory. Watch a child counting 'high numbers' and listen for the characteristic sing-song 'twenty *nine* ...thirty'. That pause in the middle is the point where the child is working out the *-ty* rule that will generate the next ten numbers.

Number symbols

Children at this stage can usually **recognise numbers** and name them. They are often interested in writing or mark-making and this interest can extend to writing quantities. However, they don't usually reproduce numerals accurately and they may use their **own** personal **symbols** instead of the conventional forms. Some children are fascinated by number symbols, especially if they have favourite numbers, and they will play with them long before they understand the connections that we make between numerals and quantity. They see written numbers on cards, buses, front doors and lifts, and if these are discussed they'll soon learn to recognise them.

Computers and calculators give children lots of opportunities to play with numbers. (See *Calculator calls*, page 21.) They often develop a fascination for long strings of numbers around the same time as they start to try their hand at pretend writing. All this playful experience of written numbers is important, as it takes children a long time to connect numerals with amounts.

How an adult can help

Children at this level can usually continue and prolong a theme without adult support. They are beginning to apply rules to number activity and they can be helped by **structured activities** that give them a particular role to play. Adults can help these children by providing number activities in structured games and pretend play. (See *Bear races*, page 47.) The structure of the games demonstrates the function of counting to the children, while the roles involved in such games give children a social motivation to count and write.

Independent stage

Number and counting

At this level, children are beginning to use numbers to do things for themselves. They have a good enough grasp of what number is about to turn it to their own purposes – whether to justify themselves in argument or to work out how many sweets they can have. They know **what counting is used for**: to tell how many things there are. Their experiences of playing with quantities and number words help them to develop a mental image of quantity. This allows them to use the simple logic of number. They can **add and subtract** small numbers of objects and talk about what they are doing.

As well as being able to **calculate** and **predict**, children can **solve hidden number problems**, such as working out how many items have been hidden or eaten. (See *Hungry robot*, page 58 and *Hiders and seekers*, page 34.) This is quite advanced because the children are now taking into account absent or invisible quantities – important for mental arithmetic and school maths generally. In the early stages, children may still depend on some visible picture of the hidden quantity, understandable, given how small their memory is. This is why you often see young children using their fingers to work out a number problem – the fingers serve to keep things in memory for them.

At this level children are also able to **spot number patterns** and use the patterns in the number sequence to count to larger numbers.

Number symbols

Children at this level can **match numerals to amounts**. This understanding helps them to read and write numerals to record hidden quantities. Their writing activity helps them to remember the correct shape and orientation of the numerals – something that it takes them a long time to get right. The relation between the numerals 1–9 and the concepts they represent is far simpler than the relation between letters and sounds, so children generally learn to write meaningful numbers far in advance of letters. Of course, it will be a long time before they understand how the digits are combined to make bigger numbers, but their knowledge of these first written numbers is enough for them to use the written symbols to solve numerical problems (See *Box Numbers*, page 42).

How an adult can help

Children using number at the independent level usually have their own very personal reasons for counting and using number. Adults can help children at this level by encouraging conversation about their intentions. The game-like contexts of the activities are ideal for developing this shared understanding.

The activities

Most of the activities in the Number section can be used with children at a variety of ages or development levels. This allows children at the 'beginner' level to gain as much from the experience as children at the 'independent' level. (See pages 16–18 for a full description.)

Blast off!

An imaginative space ride gives a context for reciting number words, and for counting stars and rocks from 'outer space'.

You will need

- model or sit-in spacecraft
- painted backdrop of stars and planets
- egg-shaped silver foil balls ('moon rocks')

> Main aims

- to provide opportunities to join in counting
- to provide a context for counting objects

💬 Things to talk about

- *Let's count to ten to launch the spacecraft. Can you count with me?*
- *What do you like to count on journeys? What do you think you would count on a space journey?*
- *Shall we count the moon rocks one by one?*
- *Can you count 'very high'? Let's count all the stars.* (on the backdrop) *Can you hear a pattern in the numbers?*

❓ Do the children...

- say the numbers together as a group?
- count the moon rocks using one number per object?
- count how many stars there are in the backdrop?

🤸 Further challenges

- Count backwards from ten to launch the spacecraft.
- Make dials with written numbers for the spacecraft.

beginner
number and counting
▸ comparing
▸ saying number words in sequence
▸ setting out by eye or 1–1 correspondence
number symbols
▸ awareness of numerals

apprentice
number and counting
▸ counting objects, one for one
▸ using the 'last word' rule
▸ counting out a specific number of objects
▸ using number language
number symbols
▸ using own symbols
▸ interest in/recognition of numerals

independent
number and counting
▸ knowing what counting is used for
▸ adding and subtracting practically
▸ solving number problems mentally
number symbols
▸ matching numerals with amounts
▸ writing numerals
▸ reading and writing for a purpose

Calculator calls

Introducing a calculator into the role play area helps children to use numbers in the situations they are acting out.

> **Main aims**

- to develop familiarity with a calculator keyboard
- to encourage an interest in written numbers
- to create numbers with a calculator

You will need

- *calculator with large buttons and large display*

💬 **Things to talk about**

- numerals that the children recognise
- how to key numerals into the calculator
- *What happens when you press the C/CLEAR button?*
- *Shall we put a telephone number into the calculator?*
- *What number has Jane put into the calculator?*

❓ **Do the children...**

- say why certain numbers are significant to them – e.g. their age?
- read (i.e. recognise) any numerals?

🤸 **Further challenges**

- Help the children make calculator numbers with sticks.
- Encourage them to find lots of numbers to put in the calculator.
- Help them display large numbers like 100 and 1000.
- Encourage them to display patterns such as 121212.

beginner

number and counting
▶comparing
▶saying number words in sequence
▶setting out by eye or 1–1 correspondence
number symbols
▶awareness of numerals

apprentice

number and counting
▶counting objects, one for one
▶using the 'last word' rule
▶counting out a specific number of objects
▶using number language
number symbols
▶using own symbols
▶interest in/recognition of numerals

independent

number and counting
▶knowing what counting is used for
▶adding and subtracting practically
▶solving number problems mentally
number symbols
▶matching numerals with amounts
▶writing numerals
▶reading and writing for a purpose

Emergency 999

Tell a story about hearing a siren and then seeing the reason for it – perhaps a break-in or a minor accident. The children may have their own stories to tell which they can then act out, phoning 999, giving phone numbers and addresses of people needing help, writing down car registration numbers and witnesses' addresses.

> Main aims

- to recognise numerals around us
- to encourage the children to write down numbers

💬 Things to talk about

- why we dial 999 in an emergency; what the operator will need to know (telephone number of caller, place of the emergency)
- what policemen need to know at an accident (registration numbers of cars, addresses of witnesses)
- *Can you write a message for the emergency officers?* (using maps, diagrams, and 'writing')

? Do the children...

- join in the game and talk about the telephone and car numbers?
- 'write down' the phone number of the person calling, and the address where the emergency is taking place? 'read out' these details?
- include some recognisable numerals in their writing?

🌣 Further challenge

- Children can describe the route to their home.

beginner
number and counting
▶ comparing
▶ saying number words in sequence
▶ setting out by eye or 1–1 correspondence
number symbols
▶ awareness of numerals

apprentice
number and counting
▶ counting objects, one for one
▶ using the 'last word' rule
▶ counting out a specific number of objects
▶ using number language
number symbols
▶ using own symbols
▶ interest in/recognition of numerals

independent
number and counting
▶ knowing what counting is used for
▶ adding and subtracting practically
▶ solving number problems mentally
number symbols
▶ matching numerals with amounts
▶ writing numerals
▶ reading and writing for a purpose

Box office

The playroom can be a 'cinema' for watching a television programme. Number the seats, and issue the children with cloakroom tickets to match the seat numbers. There is a ticket seller and an attendant to show everyone to their seats. Children are involved in counting, problem-solving and using number language. There might be refreshments and programmes on sale or a charity raffle.

> Main aims
- to use sequencing and ordering language
- to provide opportunities to read written numbers

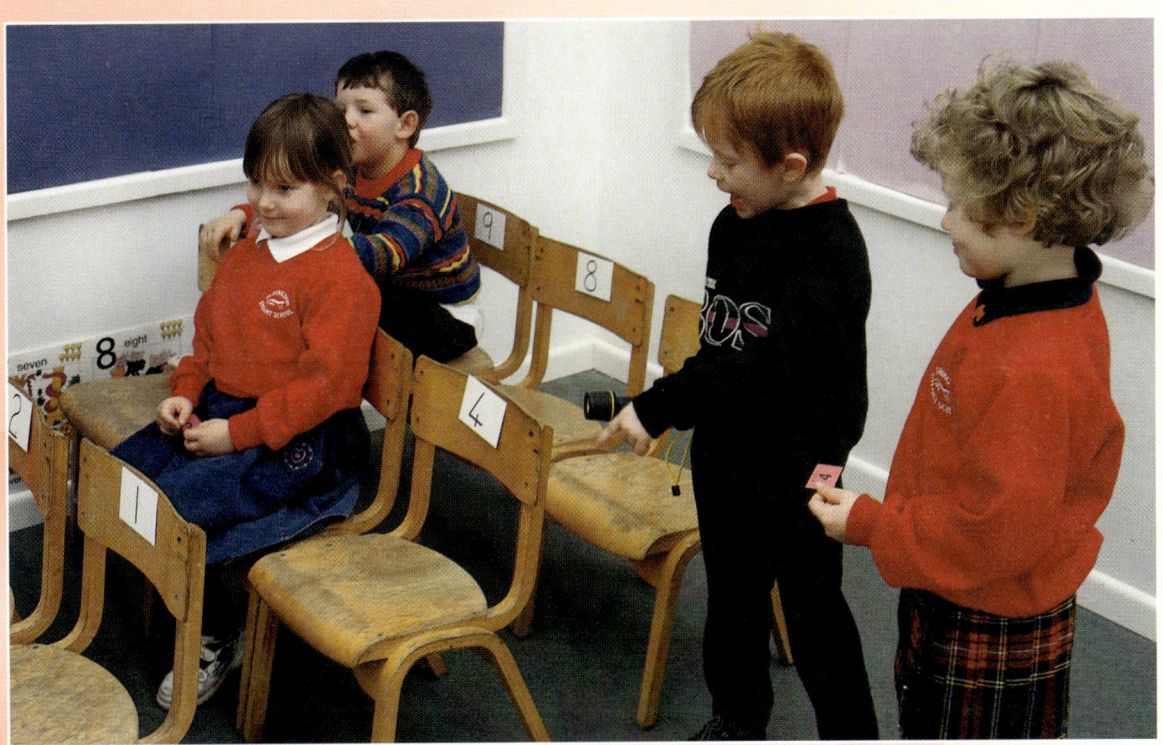

💬 Things to talk about
- how we match the number on our cinema ticket with the number on our seat
- how the seat numbers are sequenced; blue 1, 2, 3, 4 ...
- *What does the attendant do?*
- *Where is your seat?* use **front, back, end, first, second, third**
- *And the winning ticket is pink number 6! Who has won?*

❓ Do the children...
- match their ticket number to a seat?
- use mathematical language to describe seat positions?

🏃 Further challenges
- Have a map or a diagram of the seating for the children to read.
- Invite the children to draw the tickets for the next show.
- Have higher numbers on the seats.

beginner
number and counting
▶ comparing
▶ saying number words in sequence
▶ setting out by eye or 1–1 correspondence
number symbols
▶ awareness of numerals

apprentice
number and counting
▶ counting objects, one for one
▶ using the 'last word' rule
▶ counting out a specific number of objects
▶ using number language
number symbols
▶ using own symbols
▶ interest in/recognition of numerals

independent
number and counting
▶ knowing what counting is used for
▶ adding and subtracting practically
▶ solving number problems mentally
number symbols
▶ matching numerals with amounts
▶ writing numerals
▶ reading and writing for a purpose

A letter for me

Children play at writing cards, letters and invitations, or wrapping parcels, to be addressed and delivered to 'houses' in a 'street'. This gives a context for exploring their interest in environmental numbers, especially their own house numbers, and number matching.

> Main aims
- to increase awareness of written numbers
- to encourage the children to read and write numerals

💬 Things to talk about
- *How does the postman know where to deliver our letters? Do you know the number of your house?*
- why sometimes everyone will receive a copy of the same letter e.g. the invitation to the Prince's Ball in *Cinderella*.
- *Why is it important that the postman never drops or loses a letter?*
- *Why do some people receive lots of letters, and some people only a few?*

❓ Do the children...
- take an interest in their own house number?
- recognise the numbers? deliver a letter to a front door in the 'street' appropriately?
- write their own house numbers?

🏃 Further challenges
- Invite the children to look at the order of house numbers with odd and even numbers and arrange their 'street' in the same way.
- Relate the 'street' to *Postman Pat*, *The Jolly Postman* and other stories

beginner
number and counting
▶ comparing
▶ saying number words in sequence
▶ setting out by eye or 1–1 correspondence
number symbols
▶ awareness of numerals

apprentice
number and counting
▶ counting objects, one for one
▶ using the 'last word' rule
▶ counting out a specific number of objects
▶ using number language
number symbols
▶ using own symbols
▶ interest in/recognition of numerals

independent
number and counting
▶ knowing what counting is used for
▶ adding and subtracting practically
▶ solving number problems mentally
number symbols
▶ matching numerals with amounts
▶ writing numerals
▶ reading and writing for a purpose

Table for three?

Children can play at cafés; they queue in family groups to be seated at different sized tables, they can 'wait on tables' and match family groups with the correct size of table. They practise counting skills and use their own symbols to represent numbers when 'taking orders'. They can also add or take away chairs and place settings to suit the family size.

You will need:
- *different sized tables, chairs, crockery, 'food'*
- *menus, 'please wait here to be seated' notice*
- *notepads, pencils*
- *number friezes, etc. for children to refer to*

> Main aims
- to focus on comparing amounts
- to encourage counting (people, crockery, chairs)
- to write their own versions of numbers
- to add and subtract practically

💬 Things to talk about
- how café staff set the tables, counting the crockery and cutlery for each place; use **more, less, not enough**
- how café staff have to match each family to a table that best fits them *What can they do if a table is too small, or too big?*
- *How do the waiters and waitresses remember how many slices of toast and cups of tea to bring to each table?* (they write down orders)

❓ Do the children...
- set the tables, matching the number of place-settings to the number of chairs? use appropriate language to describe mis-match?
- count to match groups to tables?; write 'numbers'?
- add or take away chairs, combine tables to make the numbers right?
- attempt to write down orders using recognisable numerals?

🏃 Further challenges
- The children make their own menu, using pictures.
- They can write bills and pay them.

beginner
number and counting
▶comparing
▶saying number words in sequence
▶setting out by eye or 1–1 correspondence
number symbols
▶awareness of numerals

apprentice
number and counting
▶counting objects, one for one
▶using the 'last word' rule
▶counting out a specific number of objects
▶using number language
number symbols
▶using own symbols
▶interest in/recognition of numerals

independent
number and counting
▶knowing what counting is used for
▶adding and subtracting practically
▶solving number problems mentally
number symbols
▶matching numerals with amounts
▶writing numerals
▶reading and writing for a purpose

The supermarket

Playing at supermarkets, with a long table of goods for self-service, gives children a context for counting and writing shopping lists. Price items realistically at 10p, 20p, 30p, 40p etc.

You will need

- *boxes and tins of food (many items the same), large table*
- *notepads and pencils*
- *'money' box, toy till or calculator*

> Main aims

- to provide opportunities to join in counting
- to write their own versions of numbers
- to read and write numbers

eggs 10p

chocolate 10p

cereal 30p

💬 Things to talk about

- *Why do we write a list before we go shopping?*
- *Why might you buy not one but three tins of beans? How would we write that down?*
- how supermarkets sell some items in packs. *How can we make sure there are enough?* (counting)
- *How can we make sure we have enough money to pay for everything?*
- *Let's count our money. 10, 20, 30 40.....*

❓ Do the children...

- copy older children counting in tens? play at 'shopping'?
- write their own symbols for numbers? make lists, and 'read' them before buying?
- write recognisable numerals?

🏃 Further challenges

- Children can with help make price cards to use in the shop.
- Take turns at the checkout, using a calculator to add up the prices.

beginner
number and counting
▶comparing
▶saying number words in sequence
▶setting out by eye or 1–1 correspondence
number symbols
▶awareness of numerals

apprentice
number and counting
▶counting objects, one for one
▶using the 'last word' rule
▶counting out a specific number of objects
▶using number language
number symbols
▶using own symbols
▶interest in/recognition of numerals

independent
number and counting
▶knowing what counting is used for
▶adding and subtracting practically
▶solving number problems mentally
number symbols
▶matching numerals with amounts
▶writing numerals
▶reading and writing for a purpose

Fun in the park

Set out a park with playpeople and help the children make up stories that involve queuing for favourite rides, or matching the right number of playpeople to a certain piece of equipment.

You will need
- *miniature park, playpeople*

> Main aims
- to create a context for counting
- to set out small numbers of objects by eye
- to count one number for one object, and to count up to high numbers
- to use ordinal numbers

💬 Things to talk about
- *Do you sometimes have to wait for your turn on the swing? Let's all count up to 10 (20, 30) while we wait.*
- *Where are you in the queue? Who is **first/second/third**?*
- how some playthings are for **pairs** of children (see-saw, rocking boat, swingboat) while some are for **more** children
- why a group of friends may have to split up to go on the roundabout. *How can we make this group the right number for the roundabout?*

❓ Do the children...
- join in the counting?
- estimate when setting out playpeople for the equipment?
- count the children waiting in a queue? count the number of children for each piece of equipment?
- count up to 20 or 30?
- use ordinal numbers?

🏃 Further challenge
- Children solve number and counting problems involving 'lost' or 'hidden' children.

beginner
number and counting
▶comparing
▶saying number words in sequence
▶setting out by eye or 1–1 correspondence
number symbols
▶awareness of numerals

apprentice
number and counting
▶counting objects, one for one
▶using the 'last word' rule
▶counting out a specific number of objects
▶using number language
number symbols
▶using own symbols
▶interest in/recognition of numerals

independent
number and counting
▶knowing what counting is used for
▶adding and subtracting practically
▶solving number problems mentally
number symbols
▶matching numerals with amounts
▶writing numerals
▶reading and writing for a purpose

All aboard!

Children play at trains with playpeople fitted into separate carriages. With help, they can create 'journeys' for the playpeople in different carriages, which might be families, or groups of different sizes. During the journey, for instance, people will get on and off, until at the end everyone gets off, and the carriages are empty.

You will need
- *train carriages, playpeople, train track, station*

> Main aims
- to create opportunities to estimate small quantities
- to count a group of a given number
- to solve number problems

💬 Things to talk about
- how some train carriages are **full** of people, and some are not full; at the end the carriages are **empty**
- why sometimes **more** carriages have to be added; sometimes a carriage is disconnected from one train and joined to another, to complete the journey
- *How many people can go in this carriage? How many **more** people? Is it **more** or the **same** number as in this one?*

❓ Do the children...
- compare the numbers of people in each carriage by eye? make a group of the right number to fit a carriage? use comparative language?
- count to find out how many people can fit in a carriage?
- predict how many people there will be on the whole train? How many will be left once a group gets off or gets on?

🤸 Further challenges
- Find out how many people will fit on a longer train.
- Throw dice to determine how many people get on or off when the train stops.

beginner
number and counting
▶ comparing
▶ saying number words in sequence
▶ setting out by eye or 1–1 correspondence
number symbols
▶ awareness of numerals

apprentice
number and counting
▶ counting objects, one for one
▶ using the 'last word' rule
▶ counting out a specific number of objects
▶ using number language
number symbols
▶ using own symbols
▶ interest in/recognition of numerals

independent
number and counting
▶ knowing what counting is used for
▶ adding and subtracting practically
▶ solving number problems mentally
number symbols
▶ matching numerals with amounts
▶ writing numerals
▶ reading and writing for a purpose

Noah's ark

Children play at fitting the animals into a Noah's ark made from bricks, with stalls holding two animals. They practise counting and can have much discussion about making pairs.

You will need
- *blocks or bricks*
- *cardboard boxes for stalls, several sets of zoo and farm animals*

> Main aims
- to make small groups of objects
- to encourage the use of number language

💬 Things to talk about
- Noah's ark and the animals 'two by two'; use **pair, single, double**
- pairs of objects such as gloves, shoes, socks, earrings
- why each pair of animals would need a **double**-sized stall
- how Noah knew what size the ark should be, how many stalls to build, and how big the stalls should be

❓ Do the children...
- match animals to stalls by eye?
- count or use number language when making the stalls?

🤸 Further challenge
- Count the pairs of animals

beginner
number and counting
▶comparing
▶saying number words in sequence
▶setting out by eye or 1–1 correspondence
number symbols
▶awareness of numerals

apprentice
number and counting
▶counting objects, one for one
▶using the 'last word' rule
▶counting out a specific number of objects
▶using number language
number symbols
▶using own symbols
▶interest in/recognition of numerals

independent
number and counting
▶knowing what counting is used for
▶adding and subtracting practically
▶solving number problems mentally
number symbols
▶matching numerals with amounts
▶writing numerals
▶reading and writing for a purpose

Penny shop

Children take turns to throw a dice and collect that number of pennies, then choose miniature groceries to buy, each costing a penny. An adult or child can be shopkeeper.

You will need
* *dotted dice, pennies (about ten each), miniature groceries*

> Main aims
* to match dots on a dice to pennies by eye
* to focus on using one number word for each penny
* to solve simple number problems

💬 Things to talk about
* *What do you say in the shop when you go buy something?* (Good morning, can I have ...)
* *How much would this apple cost in a shop?* (in this game we have a silly price of a penny for everything)
* because everything costs one penny, you have to give one penny for each thing you buy
* *How many dots on the dice? How many pennies? Are they **the same**?*

❓ Do the children...
* match pennies to dots by eye?
* count the dots? the pennies?
* work out how much they'll have left when they spend some pennies?

🍀 Further challenges
* Play shop using numeral dice.
* Price everything at 2p or 3p.

beginner
number and counting
❯comparing
❯saying number words in sequence
❯setting out by eye or 1–1 correspondence
number symbols
❯awareness of numerals

apprentice
number and counting
❯counting objects, one for one
❯using the 'last word' rule
❯counting out a specific number of objects
❯using number language
number symbols
❯using own symbols
❯interest in/recognition of numerals

independent
number and counting
❯knowing what counting is used for
❯adding and subtracting practically
❯solving number problems mentally
number symbols
❯matching numerals with amounts
❯writing numerals
❯reading and writing for a purpose

Car parks

Children can play at car parks using shoe boxes marked with a different number of spaces. They match spaces to cars and compare the numbers of cars in different car parks. A 'spaces empty' board on the car park indicates the number of spaces left, and children can change this as each car enters or leaves.

You will need
- shoe boxes, marker pen, toy cars

Main aims
- to encourage one-to-one visual matching (cars to spaces)
- to give a context for counting
- to match amounts to numerals and to use number to predict

Things to talk about
- *How do people park their cars in a car park?* (side by side in the spaces)
- *How many cars can fit in each space?* (only one)
- how we look for spaces in a car park, one level at a time; but it may be full
- *How many cars can fit in that car park?*

Do the children...
- match cars to spaces by eye?
- count the cars in each car park?
- match their ticket number to a parking space?
- predict how many more cars will fit in the car park?
- write numerals on the 'spaces empty' board?

Further challenges
- Children throw a dice to determine how many cars they can drive in or out on their turn.
- Children can number the spaces and make numbered tickets.

beginner
number and counting
▶comparing
▶saying number words in sequence
▶setting out by eye or 1–1 correspondence
number symbols
▶awareness of numerals

apprentice
number and counting
▶counting objects, one for one
▶using the 'last word' rule
▶counting out a specific number of objects
▶using number language
number symbols
▶using own symbols
▶interest in/recognition of numerals

independent
number and counting
▶knowing what counting is used for
▶adding and subtracting practically
▶solving number problems mentally
number symbols
▶matching numerals with amounts
▶writing numerals
▶reading and writing for a purpose

Boat loads

Children playing with boats and playpeople in the water can be encouraged to count, compare quantities and recognise numerals. If boats of different sizes are used, the game can be to group the playpeople into different sized families and match them to boats. Children can make labels for the boats indicating the number allowed in each.

You will need
- *wide, shallow water tray, collection of boats*
- *playpeople in families*
- *waterproof marker, stiff card, Velcro tabs*
- *charts of numerals, numerals to handle*

> Main aims
- to estimate small quantities
- to encourage children to count in order to set out groups of a particular number
- to count to find out how many, and to match amounts to numerals

💬 Things to talk about
- *Is there a boat that they all prefer? What about this big one? What will happen if they all try to get in? Will it sink?*
- *How many people can go in this big boat/this little one? Shall we make it safe by having some rules?*
- how to put number labels on the boats
- *Will this family fit in that boat? If this group goes in that boat will there be any empty spaces?*

❓ Do the children...
- recognise group sizes by eye?
- recognise the numerals on the boats?
- relate the numerals to the number of people in each group?

🤸 Further challenges
- Have boat races to introduce the ordinal numbers (first, second etc.).
- Relate the game to stories such as *Mr Gumpy's Outing* and *Who sank the Boat?*

beginner
number and counting
▶comparing
▶saying number words in sequence
▶setting out by eye or 1–1 correspondence
number symbols
▶awareness of numerals

apprentice
number and counting
▶counting objects, one for one
▶using the 'last word' rule
▶counting out a specific number of objects
▶using number language
number symbols
▶using own symbols
▶interest in/recognition of numerals

independent
number and counting
▶knowing what counting is used for
▶adding and subtracting practically
▶solving number problems mentally
number symbols
▶matching numerals with amounts
▶writing numerals
▶reading and writing for a purpose

One for you, one for me

In a play tea-party children can practise sharing out food items laid on large plates between themselves and other teddy or doll 'visitors'. For instance, there may be six cakes and three toys. What will the children do if there are seven cakes to share?

You will need
- *playpeople or dolls*
- *large and small paper plates*
- *triangular and square brown and white card 'sandwiches', 'cakes' or sweets*

> Main aims
- to encourage sharing out food items
- to count out quantities, using one number for each item
- to compare two amounts and to add and take away with objects

Things to talk about
- how adults count out food to make sure there is enough
- why we sometimes share out food and other things by saying 'one for you, one for me'
- how sometimes one person will end up with more items than somebody else; use **more than, less than, too many, too much, not enough**
- *What can we do to solve this problem?* (one person having **more**; giving the **left over** item to someone else, cutting it in **half**)
- *How can we check that two people have the same amount?*

? Do the children...
- share out a plateful of sandwiches between themselves and another, saying 'one for you, one for me'?
- count out the number of sandwiches to put on their large 'sharing' plate, using one number word per item?
- count to check that people have the same number?

Further challenges
- Increase the number of items to be shared
- Introduce a second visitor so that the food must be shared between three.

beginner
number and counting
> comparing
> saying number words in sequence
> setting out by eye or 1–1 correspondence
number symbols
> awareness of numerals

apprentice
number and counting
> counting objects, one for one
> using the 'last word' rule
> counting out a specific number of objects
> using number language
number symbols
> using own symbols
> interest in/recognition of numerals

independent
number and counting
> knowing what counting is used for
> adding and subtracting practically
> solving number problems mentally
number symbols
> matching numerals with amounts
> writing numerals
> reading and writing for a purpose

Hiders and seekers

In a play house and garden large enough to hold five playpeople, children play hide and seek. A different number hide each time, and only part of the group is visible. Encourage the children to work out how many from a group of five hid while they had their eyes covered by looking at the number of 'seekers' left. Demonstrate all the possibilities by hiding the right number while the children shut their eyes.

You will need
- *play house and garden, playpeople*
- *miniature playthings*

 **Main aims**
- to encourage children to count
- to solve hidden number problems, and to add or take way using small numbers

Things to talk about
- what the playpeople like to do; what games they play in the house and in the garden
- when they play hide and seek, they all want to hide!
- *We've got five altogether. If there are three/two/four seekers, how many are hiding?*

Do the children...
- count the playpeople? guess how many are hidden?
- use their fingers or count aloud to work out how many are hidden? work it out in their heads?

 Further challenges
- Use up to ten playpeople.
- Use other contexts such as farm animals and sheds, or ladybirds and leaves.

beginner
number and counting
▶comparing
▶saying number words in sequence
▶setting out by eye or 1–1 correspondence
number symbols
▶awareness of numerals

apprentice
number and counting
▶counting objects, one for one
▶using the 'last word' rule
▶counting out a specific number of objects
▶using number language
number symbols
▶using own symbols
▶interest in/recognition of numerals

independent
number and counting
▶knowing what counting is used for
▶adding and subtracting practically
▶solving number problems mentally
number symbols
▶matching numerals with amounts
▶writing numerals
▶reading and writing for a purpose

Model street

Help the children make houses from cardboard boxes. Decide with the children how many windows and doors to give each house. Arrange the houses in streets according to size and number of doors or windows. This could follow on from a walk around local streets to take photos of different kinds of houses and buildings.

You will need
- *photos of houses*
- *cardboard boxes, glue, scissors*
- *sticky paper for windows and doors*

> Main aims
- to encourage ordering and matching amounts by eye
- to use ordinal numbers and comparative language
- to use counting to compare two amounts

Things to talk about
- *How many doors or windows does this house have?* (referring to a photo)
- *Which houses have one door? two doors?*
- *Which houses have two/three/four windows?*
- *Which houses have the same number?*
- *Where will the houses go in the street?*
- *Are there the same number of houses on each side of the street?*
- *Which house goes **first, second, third**?*

? Do the children...
- compare the number of windows, doors and houses by eye, or matching, one-to-one?
- make houses with an agreed number of windows and doors, and count them?
- use terms such as first, second, third?
- count the houses on both sides of the street independently and compare the numbers?

Further challenges
- Children can put numbers on the doors of the houses
- Make letter boxes for the houses and let the children make miniature letters with house numbers on them to post through.

beginner
number and counting
▶ comparing
▶ saying number words in sequence
▶ setting out by eye or 1–1 correspondence
number symbols
▶ awareness of numerals

apprentice
number and counting
▶ counting objects, one for one
▶ using the 'last word' rule
▶ counting out a specific number of objects
▶ using number language
number symbols
▶ using own symbols
▶ interest in/recognition of numerals

independent
number and counting
▶ knowing what counting is used for
▶ adding and subtracting practically
▶ solving number problems mentally
number symbols
▶ matching numerals with amounts
▶ writing numerals
▶ reading and writing for a purpose

Repeating patterns

Children copy or continue a repeating pattern with a small number of objects, such as two shells, three buttons, two shells, three buttons; or it might be little towers of Multilink going one, two, three, one, two, three. This encourages them to count. When children can use number words to describe these patterns then they will find it easier to move on to predicting patterns that use repetition.

> Main aims

- to use repeating patterns as a context for recognising small sets of objects
- to use number words to describe patterns
- to use number to predict

💬 Things to talk about

- how the examples have repeating patterns
- *Which patterns are made up of one item? two? three?*
- how if we count the items we can continue the pattern
- *Could you make up a pattern of your own?*
- how to use number and counting to predict what will come next

❓ Do the children...

- create repeating patterns of their own without counting?
- count to spot and create different types of pattern?
- use number knowledge to predict how the pattern will continue?

🏃 Further challenge

- Use more complex patterns involving four, five or six repeats.

beginner
number and counting
▸ comparing
▸ saying number words in sequence
▸ setting out by eye or 1–1 correspondence
number symbols
▸ awareness of numerals

apprentice
number and counting
▸ counting objects, one for one
▸ using the 'last word' rule
▸ counting out a specific number of objects
▸ using number language
number symbols
▸ using own symbols
▸ interest in/recognition of numerals

independent
number and counting
▸ knowing what counting is used for
▸ adding and subtracting practically
▸ solving number problems mentally
number symbols
▸ matching numerals with amounts
▸ writing numerals
▸ reading and writing for a purpose

Cooking numbers

The children walk round the nursery and choose a number from one of the many places where they see numbers written down. Let them draw numerals in the air and guess what the others are drawing. They can shape their number with pastry, then cook and eat it. Numbers taste extra good sprinkled with sugar and cinnamon!

You will need
- *pastry dough, sugar, cinnamon*
- *baking trays, oven*
- *numerals on display and to handle*

> Main aims
- to encourage children's awareness of written numerals
- to recognise numerals

💬 Things to talk about
- *Which numbers have you seen? Where are they?*
- *What do they look like? Have you any favourites? Why?*
- the shape of the numerals

? Do the children...
- show awareness of numerals, and find one they like?
- know the names and shapes of numerals?

✿ Further challenges
- The children can put the baked numbers in order.
- They can decorate the baked numbers with the appropriate number of currants.

beginner
number and counting
▶comparing
▶saying number words in sequence
▶setting out by eye or 1–1 correspondence
number symbols
▶awareness of numerals

apprentice
number and counting
▶counting objects, one for one
▶using the 'last word' rule
▶counting out a specific number of objects
▶using number language
number symbols
▶using own symbols
▶interest in/recognition of numerals

independent
number and counting
▶knowing what counting is used for
▶adding and subtracting practically
▶solving number problems mentally
number symbols
▶matching numerals with amounts
▶writing numerals
▶reading and writing for a purpose

Number books

In this activity children are encouraged to make their own number books, with large coloured numerals. They can look for printed numerals in a range of magazines and newspapers which can be cut up.

> Main aims

- to encourage children to read and recognise numerals
- to write numerals

💬 Things to talk about

- *What numbers do you know?*
- *What is your favourite number? Why?*
- what number they will choose and what it looks like
- whether to make a book about one number or many
- *What numbers can you write?*

? Do the children...

- recognise printed numerals?
- write numerals with any recognisable features?

🤸 Further challenge

- The children can illustrate their numeral with cut-out pictures and match the numerals to objects in different ways.

beginner
number and counting
- comparing
- saying number words in sequence
- setting out by eye or 1–1 correspondence
number symbols
- awareness of numerals

apprentice
number and counting
- counting objects, one for one
- using the 'last word' rule
- counting out a specific number of objects
- using number language
number symbols
- using own symbols
- interest in/recognition of numerals

independent
number and counting
- knowing what counting is used for
- adding and subtracting practically
- solving number problems mentally
number symbols
- matching numerals with amounts
- writing numerals
- reading and writing for a purpose

Birthday card shop

Playing in a birthday card shop can give rise to many opportunities for sorting and number recognition. Children enjoy sorting cards into 'sets': for children who are different ages, for mothers, fathers, grandparents, friends and babies.

> Main aims
- to sort into categories and encourage an awareness of written numbers
- to read numerals and relate them to children's experiences

💬 Things to talk about
- why cards often have large numbers on up to 10, and some are for people who are **more than** ten, such as 18, 21, 40, 65
- how we can make cards for family members with their ages on
- how you can read the price if there's a price label

❓ Do the children...
- talk about the numbers on the cards, using some number words?
- find numerals to show how old they think their family members are? sort the cards into sets by age number?

🤸 Further challenge
- The children can write out a price list for the different cards.

beginner
number and counting
▶comparing
▶saying number words in sequence
▶setting out by eye or 1–1 correspondence
number symbols
▶awareness of numerals

apprentice
number and counting
▶counting objects, one for one
▶using the 'last word' rule
▶counting out a specific number of objects
▶using number language
number symbols
▶using own symbols
▶interest in/recognition of numerals

independent
number and counting
▶knowing what counting is used for
▶adding and subtracting practically
▶solving number problems mentally
number symbols
▶matching numerals with amounts
▶writing numerals
▶reading and writing for a purpose

Decorated biscuits

Children make biscuits but can only use three items to decorate them. They can choose what to use from two types of decoration, such as chocolate drops and cherries. Help them to see the different combinations that make up three: two cherries and one chocolate drop, or two chocolate drops and one cherry.

You will need
- *biscuit dough, cutters, baking trays, oven*
- *small decorations (cherries, Smarties, jelly sweets or chocolate drops)*

> Main aims
- to set out a specified number of things by eye
- to use counting to set out a specified number
- to use counting to compare and combine small numbers and predict using number

💬 Things to talk about
- *What will the biscuits look like with different kinds of decorations on them?*
- *Are all these the same? How are they different?*
- *What else could we do to make just 3?*

❓ Do the children...
- use matching to stick the appropriate number of decorations on each biscuit?
- count out the decorations?
- compare the number of different types of decorations on each biscuit? predict the number they'll need to make up 3?

🏃 Further challenges
- Use larger numbers of decorations on each biscuit.
- Offer three choices of decoration.

beginner
number and counting
▶comparing
▶saying number words in sequence
▶setting out by eye or 1–1 correspondence
number symbols
▶awareness of numerals

apprentice
number and counting
▶counting objects, one for one
▶using the 'last word' rule
▶counting out a specific number of objects
▶using number language
number symbols
▶using own symbols
▶interest in/recognition of numerals

independent
number and counting
▶knowing what counting is used for
▶adding and subtracting practically
▶solving number problems mentally
number symbols
▶matching numerals with amounts
▶writing numerals
▶reading and writing for a purpose

Decorated plate line

Children can stick objects such as buttons, matchboxes or tickets onto paper plates in groups of either one, two, three or four. When they have done this they peg the plates onto a washing line to make 'one, two, three, four' patterns.

You will need
- *paper plates, glue*
- *collection of objects for collage*
- *washing line, pegs*

> Main aims
- to set out small quantities by eye
- to count small quantities

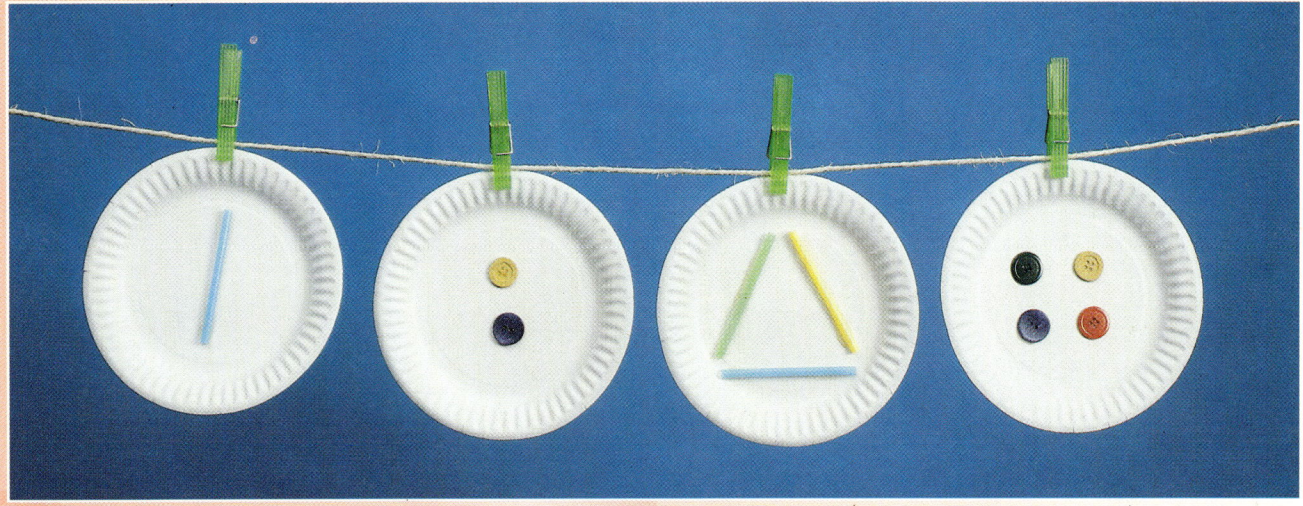

💬 Things to talk about
- what the plates will look like with different numbers of objects on them?
- *How many buttons will you need to make the pattern?*

? Do the children...
- use matching to stick the appropriate number of objects to each plate?
- count out the objects?
- put the plates in a 1, 2, 3, 4 pattern?

🏃 Further challenges
- Use larger quantities of collage items on each plate.
- Put a numeral on each plate to specify the sequence.

beginner
number and counting
▶comparing
▶saying number words in sequence
▶setting out by eye or 1–1 correspondence
number symbols
▶awareness of numerals

apprentice
number and counting
▶counting objects, one for one
▶using the 'last word' rule
▶counting out a specific number of objects
▶using number language
number symbols
▶using own symbols
▶interest in/recognition of numerals

independent
number and counting
▶knowing what counting is used for
▶adding and subtracting practically
▶solving number problems mentally
number symbols
▶matching numerals with amounts
▶writing numerals mentally
▶reading and writing for a purpose

Box numbers

Children have a selection of small lidded boxes with one, two, three or four toys in them or none at all. Count the toys with the children, and put the lids on. They can then play a game of finding the box with three in or the one with four in. Suggest putting labels on the boxes to help remember how many are inside. Then see if the children can find the box with three inside by reading the label. Remove one toy secretly and challenge the children to find out which box it came from.

You will need

- *boxes with lids, Post-its, pencils*
- *collections of small objects of the same kind (buttons, bears, wooden animals)*

> Main aims

- to encourage the children to use their own symbols to record quantity
- to link numerals to amounts/use numerals to solve problems

💬 Things to talk about

- how we might read labels to find out how many things are inside, e.g. multi-packs of crisps, egg boxes or sweet packs
- how we can write a numeral on a Post-it to remember how many toys are in a box
- *How would other people know how many are in the box without lifting the lid?*

? Do the children...

- Say how many are in the boxes when asked?
- write quantities that only they can read, or make the same number of marks as objects?
- write quantities that another can read? 'read' each other's writing in a game?
- use the written numbers to solve the subtraction problem?

🤸 Further challenges

- Children in pairs can write messages to each other about hidden quantities.
- Children can choose numbers to put in the boxes and write labels to match.

beginner
number and counting
▶comparing
▶saying number words in sequence
▶setting out by eye or 1–1 correspondence
number symbols
▶awareness of numerals

apprentice
number and counting
▶counting objects, one for one
▶using the 'last word' rule
▶counting out a specific number of objects
▶using number language
number symbols
▶using own symbols
▶interest in/recognition of numerals

independent
number and counting
▶knowing what counting is used for
▶adding and subtracting practically
▶solving number problems mentally
number symbols
▶matching numerals with amounts
▶writing numerals
▶reading and writing for a purpose

42

Jump to it!

During indoor or outdoor physical activity, give the children an action to do such as running, hopping, walking backwards or skipping. Then call out 'jump!' as a signal for them to jump into hoops (set out randomly with plenty of space between), in groups of three. The number in a group can then be changed to four or five so that children need to count to check.

You will need
- *large hoops*

> Main aims
- to make a group of a small number by eye
- to create opportunities to count and make a group of a particular number

💬 Things to talk about
- the actions that the children will do (try them out, demonstrate them)
- how to play the game of 'jumping to it'
- how many children can go in each hoop (demonstrate this)
  What can you do if the hoop you want to jump into already has enough children in?
- the difference between **this number** of children and **too many** or **not enough** children
- *How can you tell if a group is small enough to jump in with?*

❓ Do the children...
- correct others trying to join a group that's already big enough, without counting?
- Say how many are in the hoop when asked?

🤸 Further challenge
- Set up the activity with a bigger size of group, so more counting is required.

beginner
number and counting
▶comparing
▶saying number words in sequence
▶setting out by eye or 1–1 correspondence
number symbols
▶awareness of numerals

apprentice
number and counting
▶counting objects, one for one
▶using the 'last word' rule
▶counting out a specific number of objects
▶using number language
number symbols
▶using own symbols
▶interest in/recognition of numerals

independent
number and counting
▶knowing what counting is used for
▶adding and subtracting practically
▶solving number problems mentally
number symbols
▶matching numerals with amounts
▶writing numerals
▶reading and writing for a purpose

Pass the parcel

In this activity children play a party game they may already know, adapted to become a number learning game. The parcel they pass is a nest of four or five boxes, each containing a number of conkers or beads wrapped together. When the music stops whoever is holding the box takes off the lid, unwraps the parcel and counts the things inside.

You will need

- *four or five boxes that fit loosely inside one another*
- *conkers, beads or similar objects*
- *music that can be turned on and off easily*

> Main aims

- to imitate counting
- to count saying one number for one object, and to use the 'last word' rule to say how many

💬 Things to talk about

- *How do you play 'Pass the parcel' at parties?*
- the rules of this game

❓ Do the children...

- count the conkers, sometimes missing an exact match between number word and item?
- count the conkers using one number word per item?
- say how many there are when asked?

🏃 Further challenge

- When children have counted the conkers, they do as many hops as the number of objects in the box.

beginner
number and counting
▶comparing
▶saying number words in sequence
▶setting out by eye or 1–1 correspondence
number symbols
▶awareness of numerals

apprentice
number and counting
▶counting objects, one for one
▶using the 'last word' rule
▶counting out a specific number of objects
▶using number language
number symbols
▶using own symbols
▶interest in/recognition of numerals

independent
number and counting
▶knowing what counting is used for
▶adding and subtracting practically
▶solving number problems mentally
number symbols
▶matching numerals with amounts
▶writing numerals
▶reading and writing for a purpose

Don't break the eggs!

The children collect and pack eggs, giving them experience of matching and counting. Pretending that the eggs are real will encourage the children to handle them *singly* so as not to break them. Using egg boxes with 4, 6, 12 or 24 spaces, children throw dotted dice and put that many eggs in their egg box.

You will need

- real eggs, and papier mâché, Plasticine or (baked) flour paste eggs
- egg boxes in a variety of sizes: 4, 6, 12, 24
- basket with straw as a nest for eggs
- dice with 1 to 3 dots

> Main aims

- to match objects to spaces, and to set out particular numbers of objects by eye
- to count in order to set out a particular number of objects
- to use number to predict, and to add and subtract practically

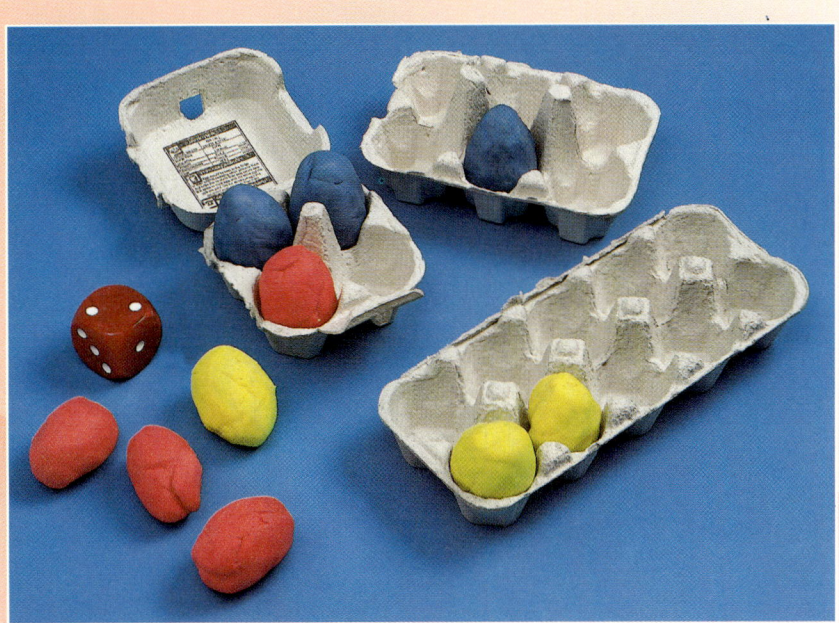

Things to talk about

- how eggs break easily (demonstrate), how we use them for food, and why we must be very careful when handling eggs, so that they do not break
- how eggs go in special boxes to take different numbers: 6, 12, 24, and how this game is played
- *How many eggs are in the box? How many more eggs are needed to fill the box?*

? Do the children...

- put out the eggs to match the box spaces by eye? match the number of eggs to dots on the dice by eye?
- count out the eggs to match the number on the dice? count all the eggs when they've filled the boxes and say how many they have?
- predict who will fill their egg box first?

Further challenge

- Throw the dice to decide how many eggs will be cooked and eaten. Who will empty their egg box first?

beginner
number and counting
▶comparing
▶saying number words in sequence
▶setting out by eye or 1–1 correspondence
number symbols
▶awareness of numerals

apprentice
number and counting
▶counting objects, one for one
▶using the 'last word' rule
▶counting out a specific number of objects
▶using number language
number symbols
▶using own symbols
▶interest in/recognition of numerals

independent
number and counting
▶knowing what counting is used for
▶adding and subtracting practically
▶solving number problems mentally
number symbols
▶matching numerals with amounts
▶writing numerals
▶reading and writing for a purpose

Collecting bears

Give the children dice with 2, 3 or 4 dots on each side. They take turns to throw their dice into a tray and then take bears to the amount shown (all the same size) until all the bears are taken.

You will need
- collection of small plastic bears of different sizes
- dice with 2, 3 and 4 dots
- tray or lid

> Main aims
- to match the number of objects to dots, and to compare sets of objects by eye
- to count objects and dots on the dice
- to use counting to compare sets

💬 Things to talk about
- how we throw the dice and read the dots to tell how many bears to take
- you can only take bears of the same size: big, little or medium sized *How many bears can you take if you throw a four?*
- how you can take **fewer** if you only throw a two

❓ Do the children...
- compare their bear collection to another's by eye?
- match bears to the dots on their dice?
- count in order to take the right number of bears?
- compare their bear collection to the other children's by spontaneously counting?

🏃 Further challenges
- Play the game using 1–6 dice.
- Use dice with numerals.

beginner
number and counting
▶comparing
▶saying number words in sequence
▶setting out by eye or 1–1 correspondence
number symbols
▶awareness of numerals

apprentice
number and counting
▶counting objects, one for one
▶using the 'last word' rule
▶counting out a specific number of objects
▶using number language
number symbols
▶using own symbols
▶interest in/recognition of numerals

independent
number and counting
▶knowing what counting is used for
▶adding and subtracting practically
▶solving number problems mentally
number symbols
▶matching numerals with amounts
▶writing numerals
▶reading and writing for a purpose

Bear races

This is a very simple board game that can be used to introduce children to the rules of conventional games: taking turns, moving pieces a certain number of positions according to the throw of a dice, and the first to finish being the winner. It also gives good experience of number and number language.

You will need

- three or four bears of different colours, dice, shakers
- board marked as a grid, one column per bear, with 'start' and 'finish' clearly marked

> Main aims

- to join in counting
- to count dots and relate them to objects (board squares)
- to use ordinal numbers

💬 Things to talk about

- how the racing bears cross the board square by square, moving only as many squares as the dice has dots
- *How many dots on the dice? How many squares can the bear move?*
- *Who's going to finish most quickly? Who's going to finish **last**?*
- *Who finishes **first, second, third** and **fourth**?*
- how pleased the little bears are to all have finished

❓ Do the children...

- count along with the other children?
- work out by eye how many spaces the bears can move?
- count the dots on the dice and use the last word of the count to count out the spaces on the grid?
- use ordinal language?

🏃 Further challenge

- Invite the children to make up new rules for the bears, e.g. they can only go one square when you throw a three; if you throw a two then they have to miss a go.

beginner
number and counting
- comparing
- saying number words in sequence
- setting out by eye or o1–1 correspondence
number symbols
- awareness of numerals

apprentice
number and counting
- counting objects, one for one
- using the 'last word' rule
- counting out a specific number of objects
- using number language
number symbols
- using own symbols
- interest in/recognition of numerals

independent
number and counting
- knowing what counting is used for
- adding and subtracting practically
- solving number problems mentally
number symbols
- matching numerals with amounts
- writing numerals
- reading and writing for a purpose

Put in five

Children can play this problem-solving game with soft toys, small animals or vehicles. They have ten each and ten in a box in the middle. They throw two dice and put one amount in the box and take one amount out. In making their decisions they may make up stories to go with the numbers they are using. They need already to be familiar with collecting objects in quantities indicated by the throw of a dice.

You will need
- *collection of small toys, containers*

- *dice with 1, 2 and 3 dots*

Main aims
- to match objects to dots by eye
- to count and to set out quantities of objects by counting
- to add or take away a specified quantity

Things to talk about
- how toys at home and at nursery may be new or favourite old ones; how some old ones are no longer wanted
- *Who can find 10 toys so we can play a game?*
- *How many dots on the dice?*
- how to use one dice to add new toys (demonstrate) and the other to give them away
- how to take away and add the dice amounts

Do the children...
- recognise by eye the amount on the dice and move the appropriate amount?
- count the amount on the dice and move the appropriate amount? count and tell you the number of toys they have in total?
- predict how many there will be after the amount has been added/taken away?

Further challenges
- Use dice with higher quantities – 4, 5 and 6.
- Use dice with numerals instead of dots.

beginner
number and counting
- comparing
- saying number words in sequence
- setting out by eye or 1–1 correspondence
number symbols
- awareness of numerals

apprentice
number and counting
- counting objects, one for one
- using the 'last word' rule
- counting out a specific number of objects
- using number language
number symbols
- using own symbols
- interest in/recognition of numerals

independent
number and counting
- knowing what counting is used for
- adding and subtracting practically
- solving number problems mentally
number symbols
- matching numerals with amounts
- writing numerals
- reading and writing for a purpose

Castles

Children spin a dotted number spinner and take the amount shown from a collection of small construction materials such as Lego or Duplo. They take turns until the bricks are all taken. Then each child builds a castle – or any construction that they choose.

You will need
- six-sided number spinner with dots from 1 to 6
- construction materials

> Main aims
- to set out a specified number of objects by eye
- to set out a given number of objects by counting, and to count objects in a collection

💬 Things to talk about
- *Would you like to build a castle? What will it look like? Will you build something else?*
- how the spinner shows a number of dots when it stops
- how to count the bricks by moving each one as you count it
- *Which bricks will you choose? How many bricks do you have altogether?*

❓ Do the children...
- recognise the amount on the spinner and take the appropriate number of bricks by eye?
- count their bricks matching one number word to each item?
- count the dots on the spinner and take the appropriate number of bricks?
- say how many they have?

🌱 Further challenge
- Use a spinner with numerals instead of dots.

beginner
number and counting
▶comparing
▶saying number words in sequence
▶setting out by eye or 1–1 correspondence
number symbols
▶awareness of numerals

apprentice
number and counting
▶counting objects, one for one
▶using the 'last word' rule
▶counting out a specific number of objects
▶using number language
number symbols
▶using own symbols
▶interest in/recognition of numerals

independent
number and counting
▶knowing what counting is used for
▶adding and subtracting practically
▶solving number problems mentally
number symbols
▶matching numerals with amounts
▶writing numerals
▶reading and writing for a purpose

Trains

Some children are 'engines' and the rest are 'carriages'. The engines have large pieces of card with numerals on. When an engine stops, it must pick up the right number of carriages. An adult has a whistle to start and stop the trains. When they stop, the carriages are disconnected and join other trains. When the whistle blows again an engine can only go if it has the right number of carriages.

Main aims
- to use number words
- to focus on counting
- to match numerals to amounts

Things to talk about
- why the train stops and starts when the whistle blows
- how the engine numbers show how many 'carriages' (children) are on each train
- *Which is longer, this 3 train or that 4 train?*

Do the children...
- differentiate long and short trains by referring to the quantity of carriages?
- count the carriages on each train?
- match the carriages with the engine number?

Further challenge
- Two trains join together and decide how to change the engine number.

beginner
number and counting
▶ comparing
▶ saying number words in sequence
▶ setting out by eye or 1–1 correspondence
number symbols
▶ awareness of numerals

apprentice
number and counting
▶ counting objects, one for one
▶ using the 'last word' rule
▶ counting out a specific number of objects
▶ using number language
number symbols
▶ using own symbols
▶ interest in/recognition of numerals

independent
number and counting
▶ knowing what counting is used for
▶ adding and subtracting practically
▶ solving number problems mentally
number symbols
▶ matching numerals with amounts
▶ writing numerals
▶ reading and writing for a purpose

Calculator fun

In this game, children round a table take turns to throw a giant foam dice, count the dots and press the corresponding number on the calculator. They then take that number of bricks from a tray in the middle of the table and start to build a tower on their own baseboard. They clear the number from the calculator. The winner is the child with the highest tower when all the bricks are taken, or after a time limit.

What you will need

- *calculator with large buttons and a large display*
- *giant foam dice with dots*
- *set of Sticklebricks, Duplo or Lego*

> Main aims

- to set out small quantities by eye
- to use counting to set out specific quantities
- to link numerals to amounts

💬 Things to talk about

- *What can we build with bricks? What would you like to build?*
- how the game will share out the bricks
- how the dice is used to give us amounts
- *Why do we use a calculator?* how we use one in this game

❓ Do the children...

- pick the right amount of bricks by eye or by matching to the dots?
- count out the bricks to get the right number?
- find the corresponding numeral on the calculator?

🏃 Further challenge

- The children use two dice and add all the dots to find the quantity.

beginner
number and counting
▶comparing
▶saying number words in sequence
▶setting out by eye or 1–1 correspondence
number symbols
▶awareness of numerals

apprentice
number and counting
▶counting objects, one for one
▶using the 'last word' rule
▶counting out a specific number of objects
▶using number language
number symbols
▶using own symbols
▶interest in/recognition of numerals

independent
number and counting
▶knowing what counting is used for
▶adding and subtracting practically
▶solving number problems mentally
number symbols
▶matching numerals with amounts
▶writing numerals
▶reading and writing for a purpose

Musical codes

Children can make up sequences of actions or musical sounds and code them with coloured units, such as Multilink. One yellow cube can represent a clap and a blue one a stamp, for instance. Then two yellows followed by a blue means two claps, one stamp.
Reading these codes involves children in counting and following patterns, predicting and describing them.

You will need
• *sets of small cubes in several colours*

 ## Main aims
• to make patterns using small numbers
• to count to describe a pattern

Things to talk about
• how it is hard to remember a pattern of claps, stamps and jumps
• *Let's count the cubes. Now let's count the claps.*
• *What actions might a yellow cube stand for?*
  What sounds might a blue cube stand for?
• *Can we read the code of cubes? How will it continue?*
  What other numbers/actions can we use?

Do the children...
• recognise small numbers of stamps and claps without counting?
• count to pick out the pattern? describe the pattern in numbers?
• 'read' the cubes in each pattern to produce the appropriate actions?

 ## Further challenge
• Children can make their own sequences with symbols and then carry them out.

beginner
number and counting
▶comparing
▶saying number words in sequence
▶setting out by eye or 1–1 correspondence
number symbols
▶awareness of numerals

apprentice
number and counting
▶counting objects, one for one
▶using the 'last word' rule
▶counting out a specific number of objects
▶using number language
number symbols
▶using own symbols
▶interest in/recognition of numerals

independent
number and counting
▶knowing what counting is used for
▶adding and subtracting practically
▶solving number problems mentally
number symbols
▶matching numerals with amounts
▶writing numerals
▶reading and writing for a purpose

Sand buckets

This is a game to play with the sand (indoor or outdoor). Children take turns to throw dice and fill that many small yoghurt pots of sand which they then empty into their own small bucket. The aim is to be first to fill a bucket.

You will need
- *sand pit or sand tray*
- *small spades or spoons, yoghurt pots*
- *buckets to take 5–10 yoghurt pots of sand*
- *large dice with 1 to 6 dots*

> Main aims
- to match items to dots by eye and put out the appropriate quantity
- to use counting to put out the appropriate quantity

💬 Things to talk about
- how the dice can tell us how many pots to put in the bucket (demonstrate)
- *Who can throw the dice and fill the pots?*
- *Can we count while Jane fills her pots?*
- *Who's going to get their bucket filled **first**? How many **more** pots of sand do you think you need?*

❓ Do the children...
- recognise the amount on the dice and fill the same quantity of yoghurt pots with sand?
- count to check what they are doing?

🏃 Further challenge
- Use dice with numerals instead of dots.

beginner
number and counting
▶comparing
▶saying number words in sequence
▶setting out by eye or 1–1 correspondence
number symbols
▶awareness of numerals

apprentice
number and counting
▶counting objects, one for one
▶using the 'last word' rule
▶counting out a specific number of objects
▶using number language
number symbols
▶using own symbols
▶interest in/recognition of numerals

independent
number and counting
▶knowing what counting is used for
▶adding and subtracting practically
▶solving number problems mentally
number symbols
▶matching numerals with amounts
▶writing numerals
▶reading and writing for a purpose

The hopping line

Painting or chalking a number line in an outside area can provide opportunities for lots of different activities. Games such as hopping from one numeral to the next while saying each number will help children to remember the order of the numerals.

> ## Main aims
> • to join in counting and notice written numerals
> • to play with written numbers by reading numerals and saying number words
> • to count on by one or two and to use number to predict

Things to talk about

• *What games do you play with numbers written on the ground?* (e.g. hopscotch)
• *What number do you start on?*
• *How many hops does it take to get from 1 to 2 ? From 3 to 6?*
• *What number do you land on if you don't stop on two numbers? Beginning at 2?*

Do the children...

• say the number words in sequence as they hop?
• talk about the numerals, recognise them or read them out?
• try to predict what number their next hop will land them on?

Further challenges

• Devise a hopping line pattern; call out the numbers you stop on and invite the children to follow your hops exactly.
• The children play in pairs, one child making up a hopping line pattern, calling out the numbers as they go and the partner following. After a time, they swap roles.

beginner
number and counting
▶comparing
▶saying number words in sequence
▶setting out by eye or 1–1 correspondence
number symbols
▶awareness of numerals

apprentice
number and counting
▶counting objects, one for one
▶using the 'last word' rule
▶counting out a specific number of objects
▶using number language
number symbols
▶using own symbols
▶interest in/recognition of numerals

independent
number and counting
▶knowing what counting is used for
▶adding and subtracting practically
▶solving number problems mentally
number symbols
▶matching numerals with amounts
▶writing numerals
▶reading and writing for a purpose

Bean bag throw

Using hoops or drawing numbered chalk circles in the outdoor area will give children opportunities to play number games. In this one, children take turns to throw the right number of bean bags into the appropriately numbered circle.

You will need
- *hoops or chalk circles*
- *numeral cards or chalked numerals*
- *collection of bean bags*

> Main aims
- to choose specified amounts by counting and to read numerals
- to use number to make predictions

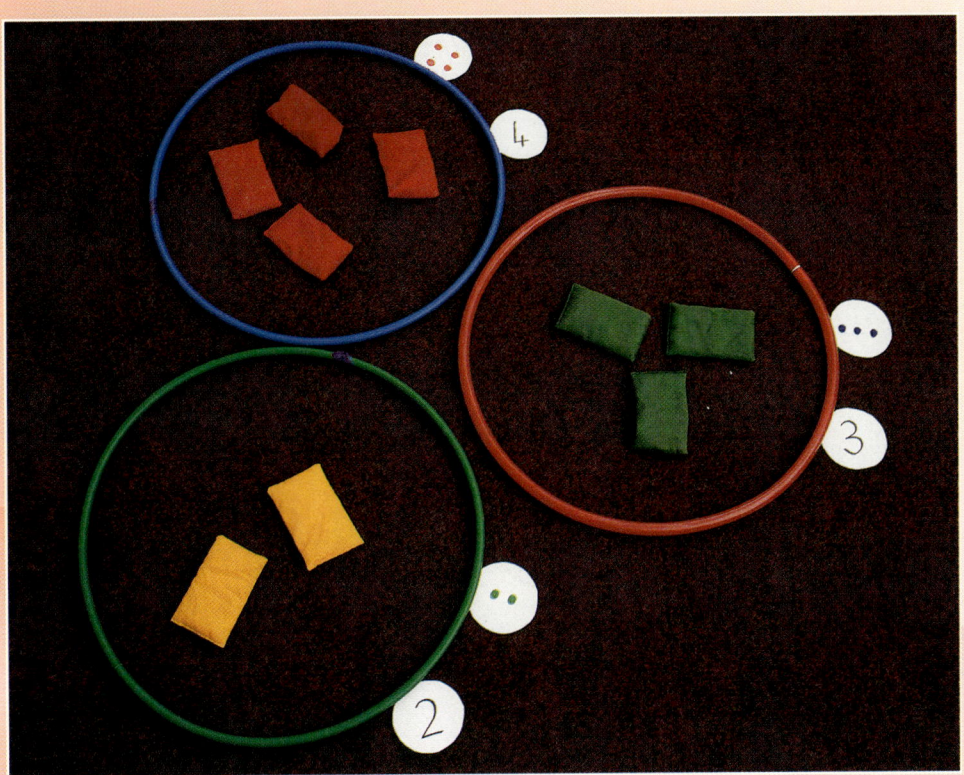

💬 Things to talk about
- *What is the number in this circle? In that one?*
- *How many bean bags do you have?*
- how to choose a circle to throw their bean bags into

❓ Do the children...
- recognise the numerals in the circles?
- match numbers of bean bags to the numerals? predict how many more bags need to be thrown in to reach the number shown?

🏃 Further challenges
- Use larger numbers in each circle.
- Encourage the children to continue throwing until all circles contain the right number, discussing how many more are needed to do this as they play.

beginner
number and counting
▶comparing
▶saying number words in sequence
▶setting out by eye or 1–1 correspondence
number symbols
▶awareness of numerals

apprentice
number and counting
▶counting objects, one for one
▶using the 'last word' rule
▶counting out a specific number of objects
▶using number language
number symbols
▶using own symbols
▶interest in/recognition of numerals

independent
number and counting
▶knowing what counting is used for
▶adding and subtracting practically
▶solving number problems mentally
number symbols
▶matching numerals with amounts
▶writing numerals
▶reading and writing for a purpose

Route march

Scatter five large numbered boxes at random in the outside area. Each box should contain items that are either the same colour or shape. For example, box 3 could contain lots of red things, box 4 lots of squares. Children follow a route on an individual card in that given order, e.g. 5, 3, 1, 2, 4, and collect one item from box 1, two from box 2, and so on.

> Main aims
- to foster an interest in written number
- to read written numbers
- to link numerals to amounts and read numerals for a purpose

💬 Things to talk about
- why we sometimes follow a route map rather than decide the route as we go along
- how the walk between the boxes can be done in a number of different ways (demonstrate)
- *What is the number on that box? How many boxes are there?*
- how the children can read their number routes (demonstrate)

❓ Do the children...
- read the numerals on the boxes? follow their given routes?
- Collect four things from box 4, five things from box 5 and so on?

🤸 Further challenges
- Children can write down a route and then follow it.
- Children can work in pairs: they each write down a route and then follow the other's, each checking to see that the path is correct.

beginner
number and counting
▶comparing
▶saying number words in sequence
▶setting out by eye or 1–1 correspondence
number symbols
▶awareness of numerals

apprentice
number and counting
▶counting objects, one for one
▶using the 'last word' rule
▶counting out a specific number of objects
▶using number language
number symbols
▶using own symbols
▶interest in/recognition of numerals

independent
number and counting
▶knowing what counting is used for
▶adding and subtracting practically
▶solving number problems mentally
number symbols
▶matching numerals with amounts
▶writing numerals
▶reading and writing for a purpose

Teddies in tunnels

The crawl-through tunnels that many young children enjoy are ideal places to play this game: guess how many teddies are hidden in the tunnels? Count out five teddies, hide a few and ask the children how many are hidden.

You will need
- *crawl-through tunnels*
- *5 teddies or other soft toys*

> Main aims
- to join in counting up to five
- to relate their counting to quantity
- to solve hidden number problems

💬 Things to talk about
- why teddies might want to hide, and how difficult it is to see how many there are when they hide
- *How many teddies are there?* (before hiding some)
- *How many are there now? How many seem to be missing?*
- *How can we work out how many teddies are hiding in the tunnel?* (guessing, counting, using fingers, remembering, visualising, imagining)

? Do the children...
- join in with the counting, but not relate it to quantity?
- know and remember how many teddies there were originally?
- have a way of working out how many teddies are missing?

🤸 Further challenge
- Extend the number of teddies by inviting more in on the hiding game.

beginner
number and counting
▶comparing
▶saying number words in sequence
▶setting out by eye or 1–1 correspondence
number symbols
▶awareness of numerals

apprentice
number and counting
▶counting objects, one for one
▶using the 'last word' rule
▶counting out a specific number of objects
▶using number language
number symbols
▶using own symbols
▶interest in/recognition of numerals

independent
number and counting
▶knowing what counting is used for
▶adding and subtracting practically
▶solving number problems mentally
number symbols
▶matching numerals with amounts
▶writing numerals
▶reading and writing for a purpose

Hungry robot

This is a 'game' about a hungry robot who takes things when no one is looking. Put four 'sweets' on a plate and get the children to shut their eyes. Help the robot to eat one or two and encourage children to use fingers to work out how many the robot has eaten.

> Main aims
- to estimate small quantities
- to use counting to compare amounts
- to solve hidden number problems

💬 Things to talk about
- *How many sweets are there?*
- *Now close your eyes and the robot's going to eat some. Open your eyes! How many has it eaten?*
- how they can take turns to make the robot eat, and the others guess
- how they can work out on their fingers how many the robot has eaten

? Do the children...
- count the sweets?
- work out how many were eaten while their eyes were closed, using their knowledge of the initial amount?

Further challenges
- Increase the amount of sweets on the tray to 10 or more
- The children can make a record of the sweets and of how many have been eaten.

beginner
number and counting
▶comparing
▶saying number words in sequence
▶setting out by eye or 1–1 correspondence
number symbols
▶awareness of numerals

apprentice
number and counting
▶counting objects, one for one
▶using the 'last word' rule
▶counting out a specific number of objects
▶using number language
number symbols
▶using own symbols
▶interest in/recognition of numerals

independent
number and counting
▶knowing what counting is used for
▶adding and subtracting practically
▶solving number problems mentally
number symbols
▶matching numerals with amounts
▶writing numerals
▶reading and writing for a purpose

Copy cat

This is a game similar to 'Simon Says' or 'Follow My Leader' but with a number element. Introduce the idea of copying actions by playing either of these games. Now demonstrate an action and count aloud in time with it, for example, hop five times and count each hop. Ask the children to copy and count.

> Main aims
- to say the number words in sequence
- to co-ordinate counting words with actions

💬 Things to talk about
- *Why is it hard to count as you jump?*
- why it's easier to stop counting as you land from a jump
- *What other actions could we use for this game?*
  (tapping noses, blinking, patting knees)

❓ Do the children...
- say the number words in sequence?
- count in time with the actions?

🏃 Further challenge
- Extend the counting to ten, fifteen or twenty.

beginner
number and counting
▸comparing
▸saying number words in sequence
▸setting out by eye or 1–1 correspondence
number symbols
▸awareness of numerals

apprentice
number and counting
▸counting objects, one for one
▸using the 'last word' rule
▸counting out a specific number of objects
▸using number language
number symbols
▸using own symbols
▸interest in/recognition of numerals

independent
number and counting
▸knowing what counting is used for
▸adding and subtracting practically
▸solving number problems mentally
number symbols
▸matching numerals with amounts
▸writing numerals
▸reading and writing for a purpose

Find a friend

In this game children move to music, and when it stops form into small groups of two or three. Playing games in a group can introduce younger children to a number situation without them needing to actually count. Some will be able to check the number in each group.

You will need
- *music that can be turned on and off easily*

Main aims
- to make groups of two or three by eye
- to count using one number for one person and say how many there are

Things to talk about
- how a group of two or three often do things together and may be friends
- *What does a group of two look like? A group of three?* (demonstrate)
- how the game is played
- *Whose job will it be to check that the groups are the right size?*

Do the children...
- say how many are in each group (up to 3) without counting?
- check and correct the group numbers by counting?

Further challenge
- Children can play the same game with playpeople.

beginner
number and counting
▶comparing
▶saying number words in sequence
▶setting out by eye or 1–1 correspondence
number symbols
▶awareness of numerals

apprentice
number and counting
▶counting objects, one for one
▶using the 'last word' rule
▶counting out a specific number of objects
▶using number language
number symbols
▶using own symbols
▶interest in/recognition of numerals

independent
number and counting
▶knowing what counting is used for
▶adding and subtracting practically
▶solving number problems mentally
number symbols
▶matching numerals with amounts
▶writing numerals
▶reading and writing for a purpose

Personal numbers

Children usually have a favourite number: their age, their house number, or just one that they like. Give each a label with their favourite number written on. Make a separate chart showing these numbers. When the children come in to nursery, they match their label to the one on the chart. This type of activity motivates children to be interested in numbers, and to want to read them.

You will need

- *chart of favourite numbers and children's names*
- *labels for children's numbers*
- *Blu-tack*
- *number lines, etc., numerals to handle*

> Main aims

- to encourage awareness of written numbers
- to foster an interest in personally meaningful written numbers and to encourage children to read numbers

💬 Things to talk about

- *What is your favourite number? Why do you like it?*
- how visitors and postmen use house numbers
- what we can do if we can read numbers: tell prices, times, dates, etc.

❓ Do the children...

- choose a number when asked?
- show an interest in their numbers and talk about them spontaneously?

🐒 Further challenges

- Children can make a collection of numbers special to them.
- Children can try writing their favourite numbers, using adult-made examples for reference.

beginner
number and counting
▶comparing
▶saying number words in sequence
▶setting out by eye or 1–1 correspondence
number symbols
▶awareness of numerals

apprentice
number and counting
▶counting objects, one for one
▶using the 'last word' rule
▶counting out a specific number of objects
▶using number language
number symbols
▶using own symbols
▶interest in/recognition of numerals

independent
number and counting
▶knowing what counting is used for
▶adding and subtracting practically
▶solving number problems mentally
number symbols
▶matching numerals with amounts
▶writing numerals
▶reading and writing for a purpose

On the move

Each child has a 'number necklace' to wear. (The number should be on a long piece of elastic so it can be turned to be read by the child.) Play instruction games by calling out, for example, 'number four, stand up now', or 'number five, stand by the door'.

> Main aims
- to listen for and notice number words related to symbols
- to read numerals and match them to spoken number words

💬 Things to talk about
- games grown-ups play where they have to listen for a number e.g. bingo, the National Lottery
- how the children can listen for their own number (the one they're wearing) and follow the instruction when they hear it

❓ Do the children...
- comply with the suggested action when their number is called?
- read their own and other children's numbers?

🤸 Further challenge
- Invite the children to pair off, holding hands with the person wearing the number which comes next/before/ is one more/one less. When children are in pairs, they may then sit down.

beginner
number and counting
▶comparing
▶saying number words in sequence
▶setting out by eye or 1–1 correspondence
number symbols
▶awareness of numerals

apprentice
number and counting
▶counting objects, one for one
▶using the 'last word' rule
▶counting out a specific number of objects
▶using number language
number symbols
▶using own symbols
▶interest in/recognition of numerals

independent
number and counting
▶knowing what counting is used for
▶adding and subtracting practically
▶solving number problems mentally
number symbols
▶matching numerals with amounts
▶writing numerals
▶reading and writing for a purpose

Crocodile

Traditional singing games and dance steps can be used as a focus for learning about numbers. Even simple dance patterns such as step, step, jump look effective when performed in a crocodile line and are good to count.

> Main aims
- to say numbers in sequence
- to make counting words correspond with actions

Things to talk about
- how to copy exactly what the person in front does, (e.g. step, step, step, hop, or 1, 2, 3, 1) and the best way to learn how to do this
- *When do people use counting to keep in step with each other?* (soldiers marching, dancers)

? Do the children...
- say the number words in sequence?
- co-ordinate their actions with the group counting?

Further challenges
- Make up longer step sequences for the children to copy.
- Invite the children to make up their own sequences with different numbers of actions.

beginner
number and counting
> comparing
> saying number words in sequence
> setting out by eye or 1–1 correspondence
number symbols
> awareness of numerals

apprentice
number and counting
> counting objects, one for one
> using the 'last word' rule
> counting out a specific number of objects
> using number language
number symbols
> using own symbols
> interest in/recognition of numerals

independent
number and counting
> knowing what counting is used for
> adding and subtracting practically
> solving number problems mentally
number symbols
> matching numerals with amounts
> writing numerals
> reading and writing for a purpose

Glove puppet magic show

A glove-puppet 'magician' makes objects 'appear' and 'disappear' with a 'magic wand'. Count the objects first, so children know how many there are. Then invite the children to predict by saying, for instance, 'the magician is going to make one block vanish, how many will be left then? or 'I had three and there's only one here so how many are under the cloth?'

You will need
- a cloth or distraction technique
- set of glove puppets
- objects to hide and count: blocks, small figures

 Main aims

- to provide a context to join in counting
- to count, linking one item with each number word
- to add or take away with objects and solve problems that involve hidden amounts

Things to talk about

- how magicians often need assistants who count things 'one at a time'
- *How many blocks are there?*
- how magicians make objects 'appear' and 'disappear' (or 'vanish') but sometimes you can see how the trick was done
- *What happened? What do you think will happen?*
- *How did you work it out?*

Do the children...

- count along with the others, but without linking one item to one number word?
- count the objects that are used, linking one item to each number word?
- talk about what has happened in terms of 'how many more' or 'taken away'?
- subtract or add one object mentally? use fingers or counting to solve problems involving a hidden number?

beginner
number and counting
▶ comparing
▶ saying number words in sequence
▶ setting out by eye or 1–1 correspondence
number symbols
▶ awareness of numerals

apprentice
number and counting
▶ counting objects, one for one
▶ using the 'last word' rule
▶ counting out a specific number of objects
▶ using number language
number symbols
▶ using own symbols
▶ interest in/recognition of numerals

independent
number and counting
▶ knowing what counting is used for
▶ adding and subtracting practically
▶ solving number problems mentally
number symbols
▶ matching numerals with amounts
▶ writing numerals
▶ reading and writing for a purpose

Who's next?

The children sit in a circle with a teddy on one child's lap. They take turns to throw a large dice to determine how many laps teddy will move along. Ask the children to predict whose lap teddy will land on next before you start counting. Count slowly in time as teddy moves from lap to lap. When teddy lands on your lap you can go and sit at the table or fetch your coat, as the case may be.

> Main aims
- to join in counting
- to count using one number word for one action
- to use the number sequence to predict

💬 Things to talk about
- how we take turns at doing things. *How do we decide whose turn it is next? How is it done in your family?*
- how the dice and the teddy can be used to decide who comes next (demonstrate)
- *Who will have teddy next?*

❓ Do the children...
- say the numbers in sequence with the rest of the group?
- count to find the next lap for teddy?
- predict which lap teddy will end on?

🏃 Further challenges
- Use a dotted dice with quantities 1 to 6.
- Use a dice with numerals 1 to 6.

beginner
number and counting
▶comparing
▶saying number words in sequence
▶setting out by eye or 1–1 correspondence
number symbols
▶awareness of numerals

apprentice
number and counting
▶counting objects, one for one
▶using the 'last word' rule
▶counting out a specific number of objects
▶using number language
number symbols
▶using own symbols
▶interest in/recognition of numerals

independent
number and counting
▶knowing what counting is used for
▶adding and subtracting practically
▶solving number problems mentally
number symbols
▶matching numerals with amounts
▶writing numerals
▶reading and writing for a purpose

Under the blanket

Some children from the class form a number line by each holding a numeral from 1 to 10 and sitting in a line in order. All the children close their eyes and the adult covers one of them (and the number) with a blanket. The remaining children then try to guess which number is under the blanket.

You will need

- *pieces of card with numerals 1 to 10 clearly written*
- *light blanket or sheet*

> Main aims

- to encourage the children to read numerals
- to use their knowledge of the numeral sequence to predict

💬 Things to talk about

- how the number cards the children are holding are all different (read them together)
- how the numbers always go in the same order for counting
- *If one was hidden, how could we tell which it was?*

? Do the children...

- recognise some of the numerals?
- read numbers up the line to find out which number is hidden? know immediately (or work out) which one is missing?

🤸 Further challenge

- For children very competent with numerals, muddle up the order of the number line so that the order read is different from the order counted.

beginner
number and counting
▶comparing
▶saying number words in sequence
▶setting out by eye or 1–1 correspondence
number symbols
▶awareness of numerals

apprentice
number and counting
▶counting objects, one for one
▶using the 'last word' rule
▶counting out a specific number of objects
▶using number language
number symbols
▶using own symbols
▶interest in/recognition of numerals

independent
number and counting
▶knowing what counting is used for
▶adding and subtracting practically
▶solving number problems mentally
number symbols
▶matching numerals with amounts
▶writing numerals
▶reading and writing for a purpose

Librarians

The children play at libraries, giving each nursery book a coloured card with a number as in a library. Children can take turns as librarian, using coloured cards with matching numbers to write down the name of the borrower.

You will need
- 'library' books
- numbered small coloured cards
- large cards on which children write the matching numbers, pencils

> Main aims
- to become aware of written numbers
- to read numerals
- to write numerals

💬 Things to talk about
- *What happens when you go to the library? Why does the librarian stamp a date in the book?*
- how we can borrow books from our library to read
- how each nursery book has a number and a separate card with that number on it
- *Why do we need to label the library books?*

❓ Do the children...
- participate in the library game?
- write their pretend numbers on the cards?
- recognise numbers and say them out loud? match the book and card numbers to each other?
- write recognisable numerals from memory?

🤸 Further challenge
- Children use a date stamp and cards to stamp the date on. The librarian can stamp each child's card and put it in the borrowed book.

beginner
number and counting
▶ comparing
▶ saying number words in sequence
▶ setting out by eye or 1–1 correspondence
number symbols
▶ awareness of numerals

apprentice
number and counting
▶ counting objects, one for one
▶ using the 'last word' rule
▶ counting out a specific number of objects
▶ using number language
number symbols
▶ using own symbols
▶ interest in/recognition of numerals

independent
number and counting
▶ knowing what counting is used for
▶ adding and subtracting practically
▶ solving number problems mentally
number symbols
▶ matching numerals with amounts
▶ writing numerals
▶ reading and writing for a purpose

Rhyme time

Number rhymes provide an important opportunity for children to relate counting to amounts. The children themselves can be counted, or they can use their fingers, either of which help them to visualise and understand numbers. Rhymes such as 'Five currant buns' provide a context for predicting the results of practical addition and subtraction problems. Children can also see the pattern of the decreasing number of buns and the shopkeeper's increasing number of pennies.

> Main aims
- to practise the number sequence, counting one for one, and using the last word rule
- to present opportuntities for practical addition and subtraction problems
- to spot simple number patterns verbally and visually
- to associate numerals with amounts

💬 Things to talk about
- How many buns are there now? Can you hold up that many fingers?
- Can we find the right number card to show how many there are?
- How many will there be when another one is sold? Use your fingers to show me.
- How many pennies has the shopkeeper got now?
- What if you buy two buns: how many will be left? how many pennies will the shopkeeper have?

? Do the children...
- predict the next number word in the sequence?
- count and say how many buns or pennies?
- count their fingers and hold up the right number?
- select the correct numeral to go with the number of buns or pennies?
- predict the result of removing two buns?

🏃 Further challenge
- start with ten buns

beginner
number and counting
▶comparing
▶saying number words in sequence
▶setting out by eye or 1–1 correspondence
numer symbols
▶awareness of numerals

apprentice
number and counting
▶counting objects, one for one
▶using the 'last word' rule
▶counting out a specific number of objects
▶using number language
numer symbols
▶using own symbols
▶interest in/recognition of numerals

independent
number and counting
▶knowing what counting is used for
▶adding and subtracting practically
▶solving number problems mentally
numer symbols
▶matching numerals with amounts
▶writing numerals
▶reading and writing for a purpose

Measures

Measures

Imaginative play

Small world

Structured apparatus and games

Outdoors

Group Time

Measures

Evidence shows that young children bring to school a range of strategies for solving simple mathematical problems, based on everyday encounters involving measuring. For example, watching adults programming microwave ovens, or measuring liquids to make packet soups.

However, children need time to develop an understanding of key ideas – the *conservation* of measures, and transitivity – before they are able to come to terms with the adult conventions of standard measuring units. The concept of conservation relates to the notion that quantities stay the same despite changes in appearance; so, even if a liquid is poured into a new and different-shaped glass the amount stays the same. An understanding of *transitivity* is based on using units, where a third item is used indirectly to compare two things. For example, using a stick to measure a line of bricks and then constructing a second line the same length.

Development	Adult role
beginner	
• Showing an interest in time, weight, length etc. • Comparing visually (judging by eye)	• Provide experiences to stimulate an interest in measures. Introduce the language of measures.
apprentice	
• Using the language of measures (*tall, taller, heavy, heavier, before, after,* days of the week, seasons etc.) • Using direct comparison (e.g. place 2 objects together to find which is taller; pour from one container to another) • Ordering three or more things • Engaging with measurement and tools	• Encourage the children to use specific measures language • Demonstrate the purpose of measures and support the children in using measuring tools.
independent	
• Using non-standard and standard measures and tools	• Provide problems and challenges.

Beginner stage

Children may **show an interest** in things which can be measured, like length, time or weight. They tend to use non-specific words like 'big' to refer to height, volume or weight. They may pay attention to measuring tools, especially those used by adults, such as clocks or tape measures, but without realising what they are used for. Children tend to **compare by estimating** or judging by eye, rather than comparing directly. They may make a bed for a bear from a box without checking the length of the box against it first, or think two jugs will hold the same because they are the same height.

How an adult can help
A wealth of experiences is crucial for children to develop their interest in measures. Adult observation of children should focus on individual

interests, e.g. a fascination with clocks. Also, an interest in measures in the environment should be encouraged. For example, the thermometer in the greenhouse; petrol pumps; scales for weighing fruit in the shop.

Adults can help children to use the appropriate language when estimating and comparing, which is fundamental to the understanding of measures.

Apprentice stage

At this level children will begin to use the **language** of measures, talking about things being *full* or *empty, before* or *after, holding* a lot or a *little*, as well as *taller than* and *bigger than*. They make **direct comparisons**, for instance, of height, by making sure two are standing on the same level.

They may begin to **order three or more things**. The sequence of time is one context in which young children find this easy. Or, in making things, they may need to make decisions about order. For example, when making a puppet, the order influences the end result: first the body, then the head, then the eyes, followed by the 'sticky out nose'.

Children may act as apprentices with **measurement and tools**, and role play using them, showing some awareness of the context and purpose for which they are used, without being able to read numbers or interpret units. For instance, a child in discussion with an adult about comparing lengths of play dough worms, might say, *'We need a measurer!'* then, if she could not find one, get a stick and mark lines and numbers on it – showing an understanding of the purpose of the tool, and some of its features.

Children enjoy measuring activities and using measuring tools, non-standard and standard units; these help build familiarity with the process and names of units e.g. centimetres, grams, pints.

How an adult can help
Comparative language is often used in stories of giants or tiny people such as Mrs Pepperpot. The giant has a large bed, glasses, and teeth... all of which can be made and compared by the children.

Children need experience of different units of measurement, for example, spoonfuls, or hand spans, or songs to time things by. However, standard units can be provided, e.g. using centicubes to weigh the baby hamsters in grams. Children can be shown how to measure using rulers and scales so that they gain familiarity on which they build understanding.

Independent stage

Although nursery age children may participate enthusiastically with measuring activities they rarely reach the stage of independently using units of measurement or measuring tools to solve problems. According to research, this is more typical of children of six or seven years old, and so the activities in this pack focus on the earlier aspects of measuring.

Baby's bath water

During the familiar and popular activity of bathing the dolls, questioning can focus on the amount of water in the different baths and the level of the water. Children are always fascinated by the water rising when they get into their own baths.

You will need
- *different sized dolls and doll baths*
- *bowls, towels, jugs of water*

> Main aims
- to use the language of capacity
- to compare the capacity of different sized baths and bowls
- to begin to look at displacement

💬 Things to talk about
- *What happens when you get in your bath? What happens when your sister gets in?*
- *Which doll fits in which bath?*
- *How much water do we need? How many jugs full?*
- *How can we measure the water?*
- which bath holds the most; use **holds more/less, full, empty, 'jugfuls'**

❓ Do the children...
- notice what happens to the water level?
- compare amounts of water by eye?
- use appropriate language?

🏃 Further challenges
- Children can dress the dolls in the correct clothes.
- Sing *Rock a-Bye Baby* and make different sized cradles for the dolls.

beginner
❱ showing an interest in measures
❱ comparing visually

apprentice
❱ using the language of measures
❱ using direct comparison
❱ ordering three or more things
❱ engaging with measurement and tools

independent
❱ using measuring units and tools

Wallpapering

Children can help paper a wall in the home corner and so experience measuring in a real and meaningful context. As an introduction to this activity they can print their own wallpaper first.

You will need
- *ready printed wallpaper, glue, scissors*
- *measures: string, strips of paper, tape measures, retractable tapes*

> Main aims
- to draw on experiences from real life
- to develop the language of length
- to use direct comparison of length

Things to talk about
- *Where have you seen wallpapering before?*
- how they will measure the wallpaper to fit the wall; use **long, longer, shorter**
- what they will need to help them measure

? Do the children...
- estimate the appropriate length of paper?
- use direct comparison, i.e. hold the paper against the wall?
- use comparative language: *too short, too long*?
- show an interest in measuring tools, e.g. suggest using a tape measure?

Further challenge
- Children can compare area by using wrapping paper to wrap two gifts – one large, one small. They can estimate and discuss the amount of paper needed.

beginner
▸ showing an interest in measures
▸ comparing visually

apprentice
▸ using the language of measures
▸ using direct comparison
▸ ordering three or more things
▸ engaging with measurement and tools

independent
▸ using measuring units and tools

74

Dinner in the home corner

Sharing out food can provide opportunities for children to explore different measures such as spoonfuls or cupfuls. Children can use any real or play food that can be poured or spooned.

 **Main aims**
- to compare measures
- to develop the language of capacity
- to use non-standard measures (spoonfuls, cupfuls)

 Things to talk about
- how food is served out at meals in the home and nursery
- *How do we measure foods?* e.g. a spoonful of peas, a glass of milk
- estimating; e.g. how many spoonfuls will be given to four/six people before the saucepan is empty
- heaped spoonfuls and level spoonfuls

Do the children...
- suggest ways of measuring equal portions?
- use the language of capacity, e.g. *more spoonfuls/cupfuls, level/heaped spoonfuls?*
- estimate quantities using spoonfuls?

Further challenges
- Children can play at measuring washing powder at the launderette.
- Help them cook using recipes.

beginner
- showing an interest in measures
- comparing visually

apprentice
- using the language of measures
- using direct comparison
- ordering three or more things
- engaging with measurement and tools

independent
- using measuring units and tools

Shoe shop

Playing at 'shoe shops' offers children opportunities for comparing and measuring real sizes. A wide selection of different sized shoes are used and the children mark the boxes with the sizes of the shoes. When the children have been introduced to the foot measurer they will need to be encouraged to use it themselves to compare their feet sizes.

> Main aims
- to demonstrate how standard measures are used with a borrowed foot measurer
- to use comparative language
- to compare sizes

💬 Things to talk about
- *What number is inside your shoe?*
- *How do you know if the shoes fit?* use **larger than, smaller than, too long, too narrow.**
- comparing each other's foot size
- how the measurer works
- storing shoes in the correct box with their size number on

❓ Do the children...
- compare foot size just by looking?
- compare foot size by putting their foot next to yours or someone else's and aligning the heels?
- use appropriate language when fitting the shoes?
- use their own marks for the shoe boxes to indicate size?
- notice that bigger feet have a different number on the measurer?

🏃 Further challenge
- Children can make and order different sizes of shoes or footprints including those of a giant.

beginner
▶ showing an interest in measures
▶ comparing visually

apprentice
▶ using the language of measures
▶ using direct comparison
▶ ordering three or more things
▶ engaging with measurement and tools

independent
▶ using measuring units and tools

Beds for bears

Children listen to the story of 'Goldilocks and the Three Bears' and then discuss the different sized bears afterwards. Children take the role of Goldilocks and make up the right bed for a bear.

You will need
- *three different sized beds (available commercially but could be made from boxes)*
- *a large, medium and small set of bedclothes: pillows, duvets, blankets, sheets*

Main aims
- to order three things by length
- to use the language of length for comparison

Things to talk about
- *How shall we decide where the bears will sleep?*
- how we compare three sizes e.g. **bigger than, smaller than, the same size as, middle sized**
- *If the big bear is larger than the middle sized bear will it also be larger then the small bear? Is the smallest bear smaller than all the bears?*
- *What is a good name for each bear?* (e.g. Big Bear, In-between Bear, Baby Bear)

Do the children...
- use appropriate language: *larger than, smaller than, the same size as?*
- order the bears by size?
- put the correct bedding on the beds?

Further challenges
- Children can make a blanket or rug for a bed.
- Make a fourth bed for a smaller/larger bear and compare sizes.

beginner
▶ showing an interest in measures
▶ comparing visually

apprentice
▶ using the language of measures
▶ using direct comparison
▶ ordering three or more things
▶ engaging with measurement and tools

independent
▶ using measuring units and tools

Filling milk bottles

Children learn a lot of maths when filling bottles and cartons and pouring from one to the other. Tell them about the dairy where bottles of milk are filled, and discuss the doorstep delivery of milk bottles, and the milk cabinet in the supermarket.

You will need
- *water in jugs*
- *funnel*
- *collection of milk containers: e.g. 2 litre, plastic carton, glass bottle*

> ## Main aims
- to use the language of capacity
- to give a context for discussion of waste and spillage
- to compare capacities directly and to order them

Things to talk about
- how milk is sold: bottles, pints, litres
- *Do you have milk at nursery? Are there individual containers? Do the adults have larger ones?*
- *Which holds the most/least?* use **full, empty, half full, half empty, overflowing, pouring, spilling** what it means when water overflows when poured from one container to another

? Do the children...
- use words such as *holds more/less, most, least?*
- interpret results of pouring from one to another?
- put the containers in order?
- suggest ways of preventing spillage e.g. using a funnel, steady hands?
- say the bottle is half full even when on its side?

Further challenge
- Children can look at labels on different sizes and kinds of bottles. Discuss the numbers on the labels: what do they mean?

beginner
- showing an interest in measures
- comparing visually

apprentice
- using the language of measures
- using direct comparison
- ordering three or more things
- engaging with measurement and tools

independent
- using measuring units and tools

At the hospital

Children use a thermometer under close supervision by an adult to take their temperature. Many children will already have had this experience but this is an opportunity to play and learn.

You will need
- *a variety of thermometers including digital*

> Main aims
- to develop the language of temperature (high, low)
- to demonstrate the use of larger numbers in a context of measurement
- to encourage children to devise ways of recording their readings

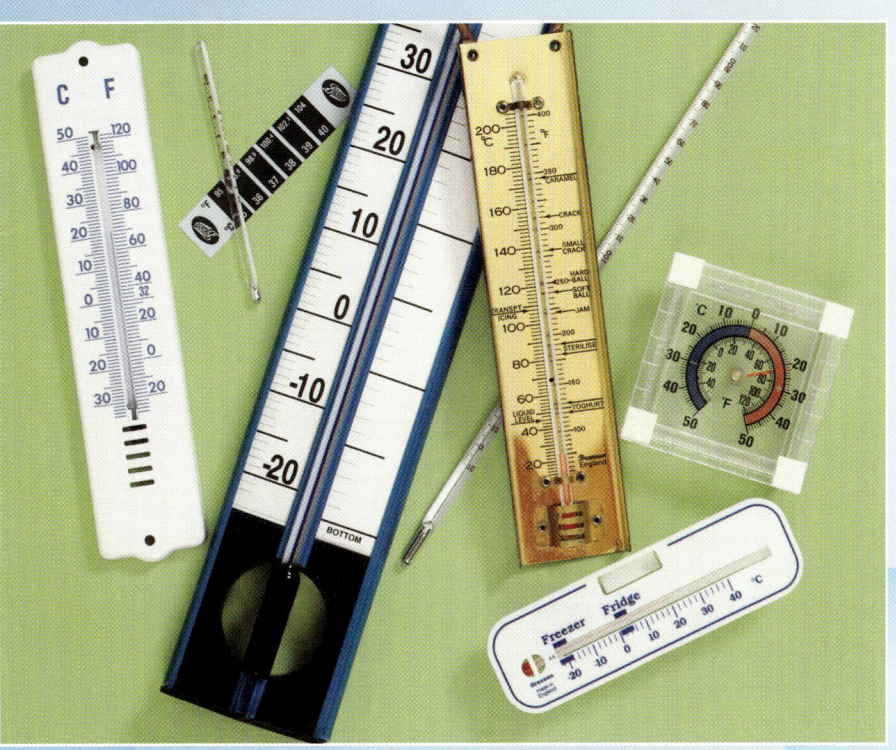

Things to talk about
- the body's normal temperature and why it sometimes needs to be measured
- *What tells us the temperature of cookers, central heating, greenhouses?*
- how things are recorded; make a simplified hospital bed chart on a clipboard
- *Why might we measure temperatures at different times of the day?*

? Do the children...
- talk about high and low readings in relation to the thermometer?
- suggest their own symbols for recording?

Further challenge
- Children can use a real thermometer for cold water play activities.

beginner
- showing an interest in measures
- comparing visually

apprentice
- using the language of measures
- using direct comparison
- ordering three or more things
- engaging with measurement and tools

independent
- using measuring units and tools

Weighing bags

Children make a spring balance and use it to compare the weight of a selection of vegetables. A plastic bag is suspended from a rubber band on a hook or stick and a piece of paper behind it is marked at the lowest point the stretched band reaches.

You will need
- rubber bands, hooks
- plastic carrier bags, vegetables
- paper stuck on the wall behind the bag, pens

> Main aims
- to compare the weight of two objects
- to order three or more things by weight

💬 Things to talk about
- *What will happen when you put a vegetable in the bag?*
- *How can you find out which is the heaviest vegetable?*
- *How far down does it go?*
- how to make a mark showing how far down different vegetables go

? Do the children...
- use the words *heavier, lighter*?
- order the bags and say which is the heaviest?
- interpret the marks, saying that the lowest one was for the heaviest vegetable?
- use the bag and elastic to compare weights of things?

🏃 Further challenge
- Children can use the spring balance to weigh the items in a sandwich, e.g. bread, tuna fish, sweetcorn and put them in order of weight.

beginner
- showing an interest in measures
- comparing visually

apprentice
- using the language of measures
- using direct comparison
- ordering three or more things
- engaging with measurement and tools

independent
- using measuring units and tools

Fruit and vegetable stall

This activity allows children to play and develop a sense of weight in an imaginary situation.

> Main aims

- to allow children to compare and contrast weights of different and similar sized objects
- to use the language of weight
- to use different kinds of scales

You will need
- *real fruit or vegetables*
- *spring balance, bucket balance*

💬 Things to talk about

- *Why do things need to be weighed?*
- things that are small and heavy, and large things that are light
- how to estimate weight; use h**eavy, light, the same weight**
- scales that they use at home or see in the shops

❓ Do the children...

- demonstrate knowledge of weighing from shopping, e.g. predict before putting on the balance?
- use language such as *heavy, light, lighter, heavier*?
- adjust the material to achieve balance; know that level means the same weight?
- explain that, with the bucket balance, up means 'light' and down means 'heavy'

🏃 Further challenges

- Children can weigh themselves.
- Use other kinds of scales, e.g. digital.

beginner
-) showing an interest in measures
-) comparing visually

apprentice
-) using the language of measures
-) using direct comparison
-) ordering three or more things
-) engaging with measurement and tools

independent
-) using measuring units and tools

Heavy bear

Children weigh a large collection of bears or soft toys using bucket scales. Begin by weighing the bears against each other using unit cubes, and then weigh three or more bears and compare their weights.

You will need
- *variety of bears, including big light bears and small heavy bears*
- *bucket scales*

> Main aims
- to show how scales work
- to use non-standard weights to put things in weight order
- to order three or more things

💬 Things to talk about
- why bears might need to be weighed. *Is daddy bear overweight?*
- how scales work. *Are they level? Is this side up/down? What does up mean?*
- predicting which bear is the heaviest and which is the lightest. *Is the biggest bear the heaviest?*
- *Are any bears the same weight?*
- *Can you find something else the same weight as the heavy bear?*
- how to put the bears in order of weight

❓ Do the children...
- compare the bears' weight by looking at them?
- use appropriate language: *heavy, light?*
- put the bears in order?
- explain that up means 'light' and down means 'heavy'?

🏃 Further challenges
- Children can weigh bears in clothes, and use different scales to weigh them.
- Use Centicubes for grams.

beginner
▶ showing an interest in measures
▶ comparing visually

apprentice
▶ using the language of measures
▶ using direct comparison
▶ ordering three or more things
▶ engaging with measurement and tools

independent
▶ using measuring units and tools

Fill a length

When playing with bricks, children can measure the length or width of a carpet by placing marker bricks on two corners and filling the space between them with bricks. Ask the children to use enough bricks to exactly fill the distance between the two markers. Help them to appreciate that when distance is measured the units have to be next to each other in a straight line.

You will need
- *different sizes of bricks, carpet*

Main aims
- to develop an interest in measuring length and distance
- to use comparative language
- to compare units

Things to talk about
- what things could be used to fill the length, not leaving any gaps
- *Is the line straight?*
- *How many small bricks would be needed if they were all the same size?*
- *What if the length was filled with longer bricks?*
- *How could we record what we use?*

Do the children...
- completely fill the length?
- use the appropriate language: *wider, shorter, narrower, longer?*
- make a record that is a fair representation?
- discuss their result? compare their length with a friendís?

Further challenges
- Children find out how many bricks fill another length, e.g. a wall.
- Fill the length with footsteps.

beginner
- showing an interest in measures
- comparing visually

apprentice
- using the language of measures
- using direct comparison
- ordering three or more things
- engaging with measurement and tools

independent
- using measuring units and tools

Forwards and backwards

Children use a programmable robot and find out how far it will go if you press different numbers. The robot is programmed to go from one child to another as quickly as possible and then back again. If the children sit opposite each other the robot can go in a straight line.

> Main aims
- to develop the appropriate language
- to develop the idea of non-standard measures of length

💬 Things to talk about
- *What does the robot understand?*
- *How far does the robot go if you press 6?*
- *How can you make the robot go further? Forwards? Backwards?*
- *Does it need a bigger or smaller number to reach Jane?*

? Do the children...
- use words like *further, nearer, as far as, forwards, backwards?*
- choose the right key to go forwards? say a higher number to make it go further?
- work out the number of units required to reach their friend? In one go? Two or more?

Further challenge
- Children use robot units marked on the floor, or direct the robot on a route which involves turning.

beginner
- showing an interest in measures
- comparing visually

apprentice
- using the language of measures
- using direct comparison
- ordering three or more things
- engaging with measurement and tools

independent
- using measuring units and tools

The bird table

Children can fill different sized containers with the food for the bird table and watch how soon each one empties. This leads to discussion about quantities and shapes, and how these affect the access for birds.

You will need
- *bird table, variety of containers*
- *bird food*

> Main aims
- to develop the language of comparison
- to compare capacity
- to order containers by capacity

Things to talk about
- *Why do we feed wild birds?*
- how much will be needed for two/three/four containers of the same size
- how the containers can be filled with food; use **tall, small, wide, narrow, shallow, higher**
- which of two kinds of food (e.g. seeds and nuts) will fill the containers more quickly
- which container empties first; use **nearly full, half full, full, empty**
- why – because it holds less or is a better shape
- how to compare capacity by pouring from one container to another

? Do the children...
- notice the differences in the shape of the containers?
- estimate quantities?
- compare capacities by pouring from one container to another and say which holds most?
- order the containers beginning with the one that holds the most?

Further challenges
- Find out what happens when you pour the food from one container into another.
- Investigate how much water the birds drink.

beginner
- showing an interest in measures
- comparing visually

apprentice
- using the language of measures
- using direct comparison
- ordering three or more things
- engaging with measurement and tools

independent
- using measuring units and tools

Sand trails

Children each have a plastic bottle containing the same measured amount of sand. The bottle has a hole in the bottom, so they find out how far they can walk before the sand runs out.

You will need
- squeezy bottles, dry sand, measuring jug, funnel

> Main aims
- to develop interest in measuring length, time and capacity
- to use relevant language

💬 Things to talk about
- *Why do we need to measure the sand?*
- whether they should all start in the same place
- how the sand in the bottle is like a sand timer
- *Why do the trails look different lengths when you all began with the same amount of sand?* use **further, longer, faster, slower, holds more/less/the same**

? Do the children...
- enjoy and show an interest in the activity?
- use comparative language?
- describe the route that was taken and explain why the wiggly route looks shorter?

🕴 Further challenges
- Children make a drawing or simple map of their route.
- Find out what happens if you use sawdust, salt or earth.

beginner
▶ showing an interest in measures
▶ comparing visually

apprentice
▶ using the language of measures
▶ using direct comparison
▶ ordering three or more things
▶ engaging with measurement and tools

independent
▶ using measuring units and tools

Planting bulbs

Children can plant bulbs in bulb fibre in different sized and shaped pots. They will see which pots hold the most and begin to learn to estimate.

You will need
- *bowls, flowerpots*
- *bulb fibre, bulbs*

> ## Main aims
> - to compare sizes, shapes and quantities
> - to develop the language of capacity
> - to use non-standard units (scoops, spoons)

💬 Things to talk about
- *What happens when the bulbs grow?*
- *How much do the pots hold?* **use full, half full, empty, wide, shallow**
- how to estimate and compare the amount of bulb fibre needed for each container. *Which will hold the most?*
- what happens when we pour fibre from one pot to another
- how we can compare the capacity of containers using scoops or spoons

❓ Do the children...
- make an appropriate estimate of how much bulb fibre is needed?
- compare and contrast the amounts in different containers, judging by eye?
- use the language of capacity, e.g. *full, holds more, spoonfuls?*
- when comparing two containers, say that when it overflows it holds less and when it does not fill up it holds more?

🏃 Further challenges
- Children can measure the amount of water added to the bowls.
- Order three or more containers for planting bulbs.

beginner
▶ showing an interest in measures
▶ comparing visually

apprentice
▶ using the language of measures
▶ using direct comparison
▶ ordering three or more things
▶ engaging with measurement and tools

independent
▶ using measuring units and tools

Freeze

In this activity ice cubes of coloured water are put into a bowl and children watch to see what happens.

> Main aims
- to use timers
- to use the language of time

💬 Things to talk about
- *What can you see as the ice melts?*
- *How long does it take? How can we time it?*
- starting the timers at the same time as the ice cube is put in the bowl
- *What does it mean if the sand timer runs out before the ice cube melts?*
- how to use the timers

? Do the children...
- use the language of time, e.g. *faster, slower, before, after?*
- compare how long an ice cube takes to melt with the sand timer?
- notice the numbers on timers?

🤸 Further challenges
- Put the ice cubes in bowls to melt at different temperatures, e.g. on a radiator, with hot water poured on.
- Children can freeze plastic dinosaurs in blocks of ice and see what happens as the ice melts.
- Make ice lollies.

beginner
▶ showing an interest in measures
▶ comparing visually

apprentice
▶ using the language of measures
▶ using direct comparison
▶ ordering three or more things
▶ engaging with measurement and tools

independent
▶ using measuring units and tools

Stretching

While learning about growth, children stretch as far up as they can and place a mark on a papered wall. If they stand next to each other as they stretch a wiggly line will be made across the wall.

You will need
- *paint or peel-off dots*
- *wall space*
- *large paper*

> Main aims
- to use the language of length
- to compare directly distances stretched

How high can you stretch?

💬 Things to talk about
- *What happens when you stretch?*
- *How can we make it fair?* e.g. tiptoes, flat feet.
- *Who can stretch the furthest?* use **long, short, as long as, as far as.**
- *What happens if you use the other hand?*

❓ Do the children...
- use the language of length: *taller, shorter, higher, lower?*
- identify the longest stretch?
- suggest ways that are fair?

🏃 Further challenges
- Children can measure each other in hand spans.
- Make a height chart of all the children.

beginner
▶ showing an interest in measures
▶ comparing visually

apprentice
▶ using the language of measures
▶ using direct comparison
▶ ordering three or more things
▶ engaging with measurement and tools

independent
▶ using measuring units and tools

Measuring a puddle

In this activity children look at a puddle and work out ways of measuring it as it dries.

You will need
- *wellingtons, a puddle*
- *markers, chalk, stones*
- *sticks, metre rules*

> ## Main aims
- to discuss a changing shape in terms of measurement
- use informal measuring devices, e.g. a stick

Things to talk about
- the shape of the puddle. *How deep is it? (over the toes of wellingtons/deep in the middle/shallow at the edge?) How wide is it?*
- *How can we measure it?* e.g. chalk around the edge, put stones around the edge of the puddle, mark on a stick or ruler the widest part
- comparing it with things of the same size
- *What will happen to the puddle? How long will it take to dry?*

? Do the children...
- suggest different ways of measuring the size of the puddle?
- discuss signs of evaporation and how it changes the puddle?
- say what the marks on the stick means?

Further challenge
- Children can see how long water takes to evaporate in different-shaped containers and different places, such as on the radiator or in the fridge.

beginner
- showing an interest in measures
- comparing visually

apprentice
- using the language of measures
- using direct comparison
- ordering three or more things
- engaging with measurement and tools

independent
- using measuring units and tools

Tapping toes

Children's mathematical knowledge is developed through music and dance, and in play using shakers which can be made from yoghurt pots. Children listen to and copy beats and so develop their understanding of non-standard units of time.

You will need
- *yoghurt pots with lids*
- *dried peas, beans or pasta*
- *tape for the lids*

> Main aims
- to recognise patterns in rhythms
- to compare non-standard units of time

💬 Things to talk about
- the pattern of beats. *Which are the long beats and which the short beats?*
- tapping alternate feet in time to a one-two beat pattern
- clapping to a fast-fast-slow rhythm
- taking turns to use the shakers

? Do the children...
- join in with the simple pattern that you clap?
- continue the beat by themselves?
- identify the long and short beats?
- use a shaker in time with the beat?

🤸 Further challenge
- Children make up rhythms using longer and shorter beats.

beginner
- ❯ showing an interest in measures
- ❯ comparing visually

apprentice
- ❯ using the language of measures
- ❯ using direct comparison
- ❯ ordering three or more things
- ❯ engaging with measurement and tools

independent
- ❯ using measuring units and tools

Shape and space

Shape and space

Shape and space

Young children's spatial awareness initially depends on how objects appear to them. Children gradually realise that features of objects remain unchanged, although the viewpoint has altered. For instance, it may take several years for children to realise that the distance from home to school is the same as the distance from school to home.

Young children can make many geometrical discoveries in play. For instance, when posting shapes in boxes, or fitting blocks together. Talking about these experiences and making links between them not only provides children with a basis for learning geometry later on, but also relates to other areas of learning such as art, science, technology, and cultural awareness. Representing spatial relationships through drawing and model-making also helps the ability to visualise spatially, and read maps and diagrams. The following table summarises the progression for Shape and space, focusing on the two aspects of **shape properties**, and **positions, directions and patterns,** which form the basis of geometry.

Children's developing understanding of shape and space may be described in three stages. For instance, children will tend to show an interest in different shapes and the arrangement of objects before they can describe them, represent them or reason about them logically. The stages have corresponding implications for the role of the adult.

Properties of shape	Positions, directions and patterns	Adult role
beginner		
• interest in shapes	• interest in position, shape	• providing experiences and language
apprentice		
• recognising and using language of the properties of shape • recognising relationships between properties	• using language of position and direction • copying and describing patterns	• encouraging exploration and discussion • demonstrating adult purposes for shapes and patterns and plans
independent		
• explaining shape names	• making patterns with rules • reading spatial relationships	• encouraging explanation and prediction • discussing problems and challenges

Beginner stage

Properties of shapes

Children's **interest in shapes** may be revealed in activities such as jigsaws and construction, in comments on similarities between shapes, or fitting objects together in different ways.

Positions, directions and patterns

Children explore spatial relationships as soon as they begin to move although they will take some time to develop the vocabulary to describe these. Pointing and hiding games reveal children's awareness of where things are relative to others. When children are arranging objects in play, painting, drawing or building they may repeatedly make the same kinds of patterns, with straight or radiating lines, enclosures or grids. These may persist as a recurring theme for a few weeks, sometimes involving children's moving or dancing in similar patterns.

How an adult can help

A variety of contexts for making arrangements or constructions can be provided, with discussion about what the children are doing. In construction, creative and outdoor play, the language of position can be introduced. Adults can talk to the children about their patterns and offer different ways of exploring these arrangements (such as printing, sticking or clay).

Apprentice stage

Properties of shapes

To begin with young children tend to use shape names inconsistently, either using the word 'triangle' for anything roughly triangular, even if it has curved sides or only for an equilateral triangle with a horizontal base. They need help to **recognise and use the language of properties of shape,** including key features such as '*corner*', '*side*', '*curved*' and '*straight*'. Constructions or drawings will reveal if children are discriminating between properties like 'straight' and 'curved', by using circles for the eyes of an animal, straight blocks for legs and an arc for a tail. They may use informal shape language such as 'wiggly', 'jaggedy' or 'bumpy', call a circle a 'round', a corner a 'point' or refer to a cube as a 'dice'. They **recognise the relationships between properties** when they are fitting shapes together, selecting flat surfaces to build with, getting two squares to make a missing rectangle or they may discover that a square can produce triangles when folding paper or cutting sandwiches.

Positions, directions and patterns

Children will begin to build on the **language of position**: *above, below, next to, in between, beside, inside and outside* and begin to use the vocabulary of **direction**: *forwards and backwards, left and right, up and down, going through, over and around.* Some children, however, will take a long time to develop ideas such as left and right.

Children may begin to **copy and describe patterns** on clothes or wrapping paper, using words like 'dotty' or 'lines'. They spontaneously make patterns with rules, but these tend to be implicit: for instance, a grid like arrangement has a 'this way that way' rule and symmetrical patterns have a 'this way but the other way round' rule. Describing patterns can be challenging, involving children in using the language of shape and position, direction and movement.

Even very young children **make spatial representations** when they draw a person with a face, with features inside the facial outline, but perhaps with arms attached to the head. Later children may draw their journey to school or make a construction of a house with rooms upstairs and downstairs. What is frequently missing from such drawings is a sense of scale, which relates to measurement, and is a later development.

How an adult can help

Children should be given experiences of handling and spotting a variety of shapes, not only geometrical ones, and be encouraged to describe them in terms of their properties. By talking to children about their discoveries, they become more aware of the relationships between shapes and their properties. Providing silhouettes of blocks and tools for tidying aware is a way of showing children how we use 2D shape properties to identify 3D shapes. Visits, pictures and cultural artefacts can act as a focus for talking about the way shapes are used by people for different purposes. We can discuss why wheels are round and roofs slope, or look at the way shapes fit together in buildings, and patterns from a range of cultures. The language of position and direction can be used in outdoor play, on the climbing frame, or on the trikes going round a circuit.

Independent stage

Properties of shapes

When children understand why geometrical shapes are classified as they are, they can explain shape names. This involves saying that a particular rectangle is not a square because it does not have equal sides, or that a 'tilted' square is still a square because it does have equal sides.

Positions, directions and patterns

Making patterns with rules involves inventing a rule and keeping to it. This shows a more conscious use of pattern which can be articulated. More sophisticated patterns found in a variety of cultures involve rules for repeating movements and directions in creative activities such as dance, weaving and sewing.

Reading spatial representations involves children in using pictures or plans to make models from, or even reading maps to find the way, and this reveals highly developed spatial awareness.

How an adult can help

Children can be challenged to discriminate between a variety of irregular shapes and to justify using the shape names. They can be encouraged to create and describe their own patterns for different purposes, such as decorating book covers or making up dances. Discussion can focus on purposes for reading plans and maps, such as designing gardens or helping visitors find their way round the school.

Bandage

Children can make exciting line pictures by first twisting up a strip of material then wrapping it bandage style around their hand and using it to print with.

You will need
- *lengths of old fabric*
- *paper*
- *paint*

> Main aims
- to experience making spatial patterns
- to use the language of shapes, properties and directions

💬 Things to talk about
- *What happens when you twist the material?*
- *What happens when you turn your hand in different directions to make the print?*
- *What happens when you move your hand along the paper in a line to print?*
- *Tell me about the pictures and patterns you have made.*

❓ Do the children...
- use words such as *straight*, *curved* or *crossover*?
- describe how they moved their hand to make their print?
- describe the direction of someone else's printing?

🏃 Further challenge
- Children can unroll their used bandage and talk about the pattern of paint on it.

beginner
properties of shape
▶ interest in shapes
positions, directions and patterns
▶ interest in positions, directions and patterns

apprentice
properties of shape
▶ recognising/using language
▶ recognising relationships between properties
positions, directions and patterns
▶ using language of position and direction
▶ copying/describing patterns
▶ making spatial representations

independent
properties of shape
▶ explaining shape names
positions, directions and patterns
▶ making patterns with rules
▶ reading spatial representations

Curvy worms

Children make some fat worms of different lengths from Plasticine or play dough, arrange them in different ways on a piece of paper, colour wash the paper, and when the paint is dry, remove the worms.

You will need
- *Plasticine or playdough*
- *paint*
- *paper*

> Main aims
- to encourage interest in properties of shape
- to describe lines in spatial terms

💬 Things to talk about
- the different ways worms could be arranged *Have you tried **curvy**/**straight**/**zigzag** worms?*
- the differences between the finished worm pictures

? Do the children...
- use shape language to describe the differences between the worms, such as *straight, curved*?

🤸 Further challenge
- Children describe the results of string printing or making other patterns involving lines.

beginner
properties of shape
▶ interest in shapes
positions, directions and patterns
▶ interest in positions, directions and patterns

apprentice
properties of shape
▶ recognising/using language
▶ recognising relationships between properties
positions, directions and patterns
▶ using language of position and direction
▶ copying/describing patterns
▶ making spatial representations

independent
properties of shape
▶ explaining shape names
positions, directions and patterns
▶ making patterns with rules
▶ reading spatial representations

Sand drawing

Making trails in sand with forks can encourage children to draw lines and shapes and to describe them.

You will need
- *sand in trays*
- *forks*

> Main aims
- to encourage an interest in shapes
- to explore properties of shape
- to describe properties of lines

💬 Things to talk about
- *Are those* **straight** *lines or* **curved** *lines?*
- *What shapes can you see between the lines?* e.g. star, triangle, house
- what difference it would make to use a stick instead of a fork

? Do the children...
- use words like *curvy, pointy* to describe their lines?
- identify any shapes they draw?
- use words like *up* or *down*?

🤸 Further challenges
- Children can make named shapes
- Use damp sand to make 3D designs
- create sand designs on card, using spray adhesive to fix, then compare and describe.

beginner
properties of shape
▶ interest in shapes
positions, directions and patterns
▶ interest in positions, directions and patterns

apprentice
properties of shape
▶ recognising/using language
▶ recognising relationships between properties
positions, directions and patterns
▶ using language of position and direction
▶ copying/describing patterns
▶ making spatial representations

independent
properties of shape
▶ explaining shape names
positions, directions and patterns
▶ making patterns with rules
▶ reading spatial representations

Golfball twirl

Children enjoy watching the trail made by a golfball which has been dipped in paint and rolled around a paper-lined container by tilting it. They can use mathematical language to describe the movement of the golfball and its trail.

You will need
- *golfballs*
- *paint*
- *paper*

Main aims
- to foster an interest in shapes and directions
- to develop understanding and language of directions and movement
- to experience properties of shape and describe these

Things to talk about
- how to cover the **curved surface** of the ball with paint
- the **rotating** movement of the golfball across the paper
- *Can you roll the ball to make different trails? Can you make a **zigzag** or a **spiral**?*
- *What shapes can you see?*

Do the children...
- describe the different trails using appropriate language?

Further challenge
- Children carefully cover a golfball with paint while holding it in one hand. Then using fingers, they roll it around a piece of paper until all the paint is removed, describing the trail.

beginner
properties of shape
▶ interest in shapes
positions, directions and patterns
▶ interest in positions, directions and patterns

apprentice
properties of shape
▶ recognising/using language
▶ recognising relationships between properties
positions, directions and patterns
▶ using language of position and direction
▶ copying/describing patterns
▶ making spatial representations

independent
properties of shape
▶ explaining shape names
positions, directions and patterns
▶ making patterns with rules
▶ reading spatial representations

Elastic stretch

The children stretch elastic bands around wooden off-cuts, and when there are enough bands to make a pattern, use them as printing blocks.

You will need
- *wood off-cuts*
- *elastic bands*
- *paint*
- *paper*

> Main aims
- to encourage interest in shapes and spatial relationships
- to experience and discuss properties of shape, especially straight line crossings
- to identify and describe patterns

Things to talk about
- *What straight lines and crossing points can you see?*
- *What about straight-sided shapes?* (**triangles** and **rectangles**)
- *What features do these shapes have?* (e.g. **straight sides**, number of **corners**, **right angles** or '**square corners**')

? Do the children...
- notice where two or more lines cross in their pattern?
- identify shapes they know, and describe their features?
- identify repeating patterns?

Further challenge
- Children can try to explain how they know what a shape is, for instance, a triangle has **three sides** or a square has **four equal sides** and **four right angles**.

beginner
properties of shape
▶ interest in shapes
positions, directions and patterns
▶ interest in positions, directions and patterns

apprentice
properties of shape
▶ recognising/using language
▶ recognising relationships between properties
positions, directions and patterns
▶ using language of position and direction
▶ copying/describing patterns
▶ making spatial representations

independent
properties of shape
▶ explaining shape names
positions, directions and patterns
▶ making patterns with rules
▶ reading spatial representations

Button up

Sticking buttons onto plastic lids or cardboard shapes provides a context for children to fit shapes together and fill spaces, as well as considering the shapes left in the gaps.

You will need

- *buttons (cut from old clothes)*
- *glue*
- *cardboard shapes or plastic lids*

> Main aims

- to encourage interest in properties of shapes
- to experience and discuss the relationship between properties of shapes

💬 Things to talk about

- how the buttons fit together, and the shapes they leave in between
- *Can you guess which buttons came from the same dress or jacket? How do you know?*
- *Which buttons would be best to fit on this cardboard shape?*

❓ Do the children...

- cover the shape with the buttons?
- talk about how the buttons fit together, or what shapes they leave in between?

🦴 Further challenges

- Children can sort the buttons according to shape.
- They can fit plastic shapes together to cover a tray.

beginner
properties of shape
❯ interest in shapes
positions, directions and patterns
❯ interest in positions, directions and patterns

apprentice
properties of shape
❯ recognising/using language
❯ recognising relationships between properties
positions, directions and patterns
❯ using language of position and direction
❯ copying/describing patterns
❯ making spatial representations

independent
properties of shape
❯ explaining shape names
positions, directions and patterns
❯ making patterns with rules
❯ reading spatial representations

Building towers

The children build towers from a selected range of solid shapes, possibly after looking at photographs of tall buildings such as castles and lighthouses, or after a suitable story. As children choose shapes, they make discoveries about their properties.

You will need
- *construction materials: packets and boxes or wooden blocks, including some with curved sides*

> Main aims
- to investigate and use the properties of 3D shapes
- to find relationships between shapes
- to use language of shape and properties

💬 Things to talk about
- *Which blocks are good for building towers? Which are not so good? Why?*
- the names of shapes: **cylinder, sphere, cube, cuboid**
- the properties of the shapes; use **straight, curved, corner, arch, slope**
- the positions of blocks; use **on top of, underneath, between, next to**

❓ Do the children...
- use trial and error to select blocks?
- select appropriate blocks or use trial and error?
- say why they have chosen their blocks?
- use the language of shape and properties?

🏃 Further challenge
- Children build bridges, discussing the best blocks for the span and for supports.

beginner
properties of shape
▶ interest in shapes
positions, directions and patterns
▶ interest in positions, directions and patterns

apprentice
properties of shape
▶ recognising/using language
▶ recognising relationships between properties
positions, directions and patterns
▶ using language of position and direction
▶ copying/describing patterns
▶ making spatial representations

independent
properties of shape
▶ explaining shape names
positions, directions and patterns
▶ making patterns with rules
▶ reading spatial representations

104

Potato roll

The children draw, then carve a design all around the widest part of a potato. Pushing two small pencils or sticks into either end of the potato, they turn it into a pattern roller.

> Main aims

- to experience creating continuous patterns
- to develop language of direction and shape

You will need
- *paint*
- *potatoes*
- *knives or sharp implements*
- *sticks or small pencils*
- *paper*

💬 Things to talk about

- how we can make the pattern finish where it started
- the directions used to roll potatoes (e.g. **across, up and down, around**)
- the designs and the patterns made: **spots** or **lines**, **straight** or **zigzag**
- how the patterns relate to the design *What is the same or different?*
  Why is the pattern continuous?

❓ Do the children...

- use the language of shape and direction to describe designs and patterns, *wavy, round, spotty* as well as *spiral* or *zigzag*?
- talk about the pattern being continuous: 'going on and on'?
- talk about similarities and differences?

🏃 Further challenge

- Children can use a bicycle wheel or different pastry wheels and run them through flour to make a print pattern.

beginner
properties of shape
▶ interest in shapes
positions, directions and patterns
▶ interest in positions, directions and patterns

apprentice
properties of shape
▶ recognising/using language
▶ recognising relationships between properties
positions, directions and patterns
▶ using language of position and direction
▶ copying/describing patterns
▶ making spatial representations

independent
properties of shape
▶ explaining shape names
positions, directions and patterns
▶ making patterns with rules
▶ reading spatial representations

Gift boxes

Children make gift boxes by carefully opening up a box to make a flat net (a shape which will fold into a 3D shape), decorating the inner side, and sticking it back together, decorated side out, when it is dry.

You will need
- *boxes: food cartons, chocolate boxes*
- *collage materials*
- *paint*
- *printing materials or gift wrap paper*
- *glue and tape*

> Main aims
- to experience the properties of shape, in particular the way 2D shapes are arranged to make the faces of 3D shapes
- to learn names of 2D and 3D shapes
- to use positional language

Things to talk about
- the names of the 3D and 2D shapes: **cube, cuboid, pyramid; square, triangle, rectangle**
- how the shapes fit together; use language of properties: **corner, edge, face**
- how the net is folded; use language of position: **top, bottom, over, under, inside, outside**
- the best way of cutting the boxes

? Do the children...
- use names of shapes and language of properties, like **edge** and **corner**?
- confidently fold the net back into the 3D shape?

Further challenge
- Children can make gift cartons of more complex shapes, such as hexagonal or triangular prisms. (Prisms are 3D shapes with the same size and shape face at either end.)

beginner
properties of shape
▶ interest in shapes
positions, directions and patterns
▶ interest in positions, directions and patterns

apprentice
properties of shape
▶ recognising/using language
▶ recognising relationships between properties
positions, directions and patterns
▶ using language of position and direction
▶ copying/describing patterns
▶ making spatial representations

independent
properties of shape
▶ explaining shape names
positions, directions and patterns
▶ making patterns with rules
▶ reading spatial representations

Outside edge

Children choose little boxes and investigate ways of putting the boxes together to fill a 3D frame. The frame can be made by taking a section from a cardboard box

> Main aim

- to investigate fitting together 3D shapes

You will need
- *cardboard boxes, ends removed and thickly sliced*
- *a selection of small boxes*
- *glue*
- *paint*

💬 Things to talk about

- the frame and how it is to be filled
- *Which shapes would fit together inside the frame?*
- *Supposing there was a space left over in the frame?*

? Do the children...

- describe the shape properties of their frame, the number of sides?
- try different ways of fitting the boxes together?

🏃 Further challenge

- Children can try to make a 3D triangular frame.

beginner
properties of shape
▶ interest in shapes
positions, directions and patterns
▶ interest in positions, directions and patterns

apprentice
properties of shape
▶ recognising/using language
▶ recognising relationships between properties
positions, directions and patterns
▶ using language of position and direction
▶ copying/describing patterns
▶ making spatial representations

independent
properties of shape
▶ explaining shape names
positions, directions and patterns
▶ making patterns with rules
▶ reading spatial representations

Russian dolls

Children make their own set of 'Russian dolls' by nesting boxes of similar shape inside each other, and decorating them. Russian dolls are a good example of the same 3D shape in different sizes.

You will need
- *a set of 2 or 3 Russian dolls, or other sets of nesting boxes*
- *cardboard boxes, packets and tubes of different sizes which will nest*

> Main aims
- to recognise 3D shapes with the same properties
- to use the language of shape

💬 Things to talk about
- how one shape fits inside another; use 3D shape names: **cylinder, cube, cuboid**
- *What is the same about these shapes?* (e.g. **square faces, round edges, numbers of corners**)
- putting the shapes in order of size. *Which is the **biggest**/**next biggest?***

? Do the children...
- choose packets with openings of the same shape, rather than trial and error?
- use language about shapes and properties, such as *round, edges* and *corners*?

🏃 Further challenge
- Children put three or more dolls in size order in a line.

beginner
properties of shape
❯ interest in shapes
positions, directions and patterns
❯ interest in positions, directions and patterns

apprentice
properties of shape
❯ recognising/using language
❯ recognising relationships between properties
positions, directions and patterns
❯ using language of position and direction
❯ copying/describing patterns
❯ making spatial representations

independent
properties of shape
❯ explaining shape names
positions, directions and patterns
❯ making patterns with rules
❯ reading spatial representations

Elephant lift

Children make an 'elephant lift' in the form of a box framework made of paper batons, which fits around a toy elephant. They make a base from card and attach string to the top of the frame.

You will need
- *toy elephant*
- *batons made from diagonally-rolled and taped sheets of newspaper*
- *card for base*
- *string*

> Main aims
- to experience of the properties of shapes, in particular the edges of 3D shapes
- to relate the shapes of two objects

Things to talk about
- what the best shape is for an elephant lift
- the number of batons needed for the edges of the lift
- *What shape will you need for the card base?*

? Do the children...
- show interest in deciding the lift shape?
- know how to find out how many paper batons to use (referring to actual 3D shapes)?
- name the shape of the base?

Further challenge
- Children make a box for two or three toy elephants.

beginner
properties of shape
▷ interest in shapes
positions, directions and patterns
▷ interest in positions, directions and patterns

apprentice
properties of shape
▷ recognising/using language
▷ recognising relationships between properties
positions, directions and patterns
▷ using language of position and direction
▷ copying/describing patterns
▷ making spatial representations

independent
properties of shape
▷ explaining shape names
positions, directions and patterns
▷ making patterns with rules
▷ reading spatial representations

Dishcloth design

Children weave various linear materials (some with beads threaded on) through large, open-weave dishcloths. They experience creating patterns by repeated movements and discuss the effects of their actions and choice of fabrics.

Main aims

- to experience patterns involving direction
- to create patterns with a rule

Things to talk about

- the weave of jumpers and fabric, and the dishcloth: **up and down, left and right**
- how patterns are made by repeating the actions of **in and out, under and over**
- which direction to weave in: **left to right, right to left, bottom to top**
- how to create more pattern with colours or materials
- *What is your pattern like? How did you weave it? Why did you choose those materials?*

Do the children...

- use directional language?
- describe their pattern?
- make regular weavings or symmetrical patterning?

Further challenge

- Children can make and describe a collection of weaving patterns.

beginner
properties of shape
▶ interest in shapes
positions, directions and patterns
▶ interest in positions, directions and patterns

apprentice
properties of shape
▶ recognising/using language
▶ recognising relationships between properties
positions, directions and patterns
▶ using language of position and direction
▶ copying/describing patterns
▶ making spatial representations

independent
properties of shape
▶ explaining shape names
positions, directions and patterns
▶ making patterns with rules
▶ reading spatial representations

Ribbon plait

Children make giant plaited streamers using an over and under pattern, as used for plaiting hair. One child is a 'holder', holding one end of the streamers and others are the 'movers'.

You will need
- *long ribbons or crépe paper strips*

Main aim
- to experience and discuss pattern in movement and direction

Things to talk about
- the children's experiences of plaiting. *What do you say as you plait?*
- *How will you know if the pattern is working out? What kind of pattern are you making?*

Do the children...
- use the directions of *over and under*?
- recognise the plaiting pattern and spot any 'mistakes'?

Further challenge
- Children can make plaits on their own, with a variety of different materials.

beginner
properties of shape
▶ interest in shapes
positions, directions and patterns
▶ interest in positions, directions and patterns

apprentice
properties of shape
▶ recognising/using language
▶ recognising relationships between properties
positions, directions and patterns
▶ using language of position and direction
▶ copying/describing patterns
▶ making spatial representations

independent
properties of shape
▶ explaining shape names
positions, directions and patterns
▶ making patterns with rules
▶ reading spatial representations

Shiny shapes

Children guess which of a selection of objects was used to make a tin foil shape, made by covering an object in tin foil and then removing it, leaving an impression of the original. Children then draw their guessed object.

You will need
- *tin foil*
- *selection of objects: either contrasting e.g. telephone and toy elephant, or similar e.g. boxes*

> Main aims
- to use the language of shape properties
- to recognise shape properties of everyday objects

💬 Things to talk about
- *What happens when you cover shapes with foil?*
- *How do you know which object was used to make the shape? Does it have **curved** or **straight edges**? How many **corners**?*

❓ Do the children...
- use appropriate language, such as *round, pointy* as well as *curved* or *straight edges*?
- draw the key features of objects?

🤸 Further challenge
- Children can use damp sand to fill up objects and turn out different shapes.

beginner
properties of shape
❭ interest in shapes
positions, directions and patterns
❭ interest in positions, directions and patterns

apprentice
properties of shape
❭ recognising/using language
❭ recognising relationships between properties
positions, directions and patterns
❭ using language of position and direction
❭ copying/describing patterns
❭ making spatial representations

independent
properties of shape
❭ explaining shape names
positions, directions and patterns
❭ making patterns with rules
❭ reading spatial representations

Symmetrical patterns

Children work in pairs to build up a pattern where one half is a reflection of the other, i.e. with mirror symmetry. They take turns to put shapes on either side of the dividing line. Start the pattern with a few shapes on each side, and show the children the reflection in a mirror held on the line.

You will need
- *mirrors*
- *pegs and peg board*, or *baseboard for pattern tiles or Duplo*, or *gummed paper shapes and a large piece of paper, all with a dividing line*

> Main aim
- to experience spatial patterns, especially using reflective or 'mirror' symmetry

💬 Things to talk about
- *What is a reflection? How do you know where to put a shape to make one side of the pattern 'the same but the other way round'?*
- the shape names and language of position: **next to, on top of, above, under, at the side of**
- how some shapes fit together and leave no gaps, while others make shapes in the gaps

❓ Do the children...
- use words like *next to, below, above?*
- create a reflected pattern, partially or wholly?
- predict, e.g. *We need a red square to go there?*

🏃 Further challenge
- One piece of a pattern is removed while children close their eyes, then try to identify it. Then two pieces are, 'swapped' leaving no gap; they try to spot what has been done.

beginner
properties of shape
❱ interest in shapes
positions, directions and patterns
❱ interest in positions, directions and patterns

apprentice
properties of shape
❱ recognising/using language
❱ recognising relationships between properties
positions, directions and patterns
❱ using language of position and direction
❱ copying/describing patterns
❱ making spatial representations

independent
properties of shape
❱ explaining shape names
positions, directions and patterns
❱ making patterns with rules
❱ reading spatial representations

Wall hanging

Children use different materials to make a large wall hanging. They sort a varied collection of small pieces of fabric, then design and make the wall hanging with their selection.

> Main aims

- to experience and discuss relationships between shapes
- to represent shapes by drawing designs involving shapes and positions

💬 Things to talk about

- *How shall we sort the fabrics?*
- *What will the hanging look like? Which fabrics will you use? Where will you put them?*
- dividing the hanging into different areas
- *How will you draw a design for the hanging?*
- what fabrics to use and how to indicate these on the design plan
- which children will be responsible for each part of the design

❓ Do the children...

- make suggestions on how to divide up the space, using language of position, shape and pattern?
- draw a feasible design?

🌱 Further challenge

- Children can design individual patterned collages.

beginner
properties of shape
❯ interest in shapes
positions, directions and patterns
❯ interest in positions, directions and patterns

apprentice
properties of shape
❯ recognising/using language
❯ recognising relationships between properties
positions, directions and patterns
❯ using language of position and direction
❯ copying/describing patterns
❯ making spatial representations

independent
properties of shape
❯ explaining shape names
positions, directions and patterns
❯ making patterns with rules
❯ reading spatial representations

Find the shape

In a large indoor or outdoor space, some giant 2D shapes are spread about. The adult calls the shape name and children find the right one and stand round or sit on it. Later a child can be the 'caller'.

You will need
- *shapes (circles, triangles, squares, rectangles) made from brightly coloured plastic, cloth or carpet, large enough for children to stand or sit on*

> Main aims
- to foster an interest in shapes
- to introduce children to the names and properties of 2D shapes
- to experience and discuss the properties of large-scale shapes

💬 Things to talk about
- *What are the names of these shapes?*
- the shapes' properties: numbers of **corners, sides, straight** and **curved** sides
- while walking round each shape, describe the shape properties

❓ Do the children...
- identify the right shape?
- identify sides and corners?
- describe *curved* and *straight lines*, numbers of *corners* and *sides*?

🏃 Further challenges
- Children find out how many of them will fit along the shape sides and discuss *longer than* and *shorter than*, and *same length as*.
- Children look at the shapes when folded into other shapes (such as triangles within the square). They say which shape is which when they are all folded into triangles.

beginner
properties of shape
▶ interest in shapes
positions, directions and patterns
▶ interest in positions, directions and patterns

apprentice
properties of shape
▶ recognising/using language
▶ recognising relationships between properties
positions, directions and patterns
▶ using language of position and direction
▶ copying/describing patterns
▶ making spatial representations

independent
properties of shape
▶ explaining shape names
positions, directions and patterns
▶ making patterns with rules
▶ reading spatial representations

Shape snake

Children play at building a snake with plastic shapes which are first shared out. They decide what shape the snake's head will be, then take turns to choose a shape to make the snake's body.

You will need

- *coloured plastic or wooden shapes, including triangles, circles and squares*

> Main aims

- to promote interest in shape names
- to encourage familiarity with shape names

○ Things to talk about

- *What colour and shape will the head be?*
- whether to have, e.g. all the triangles first, or if it should be up to the child whose turn it is
- *Tell me about the snake now you've finished it.*

? Do the children...

- name the shapes?
- justify their choice of shape?
- describe the snake?

☆ Further challenge

- Children can use a shape dice to select shapes to make a snake.

beginner
properties of shape
▶ interest in shapes
positions, directions and patterns
▶ interest in positions, directions and patterns

apprentice
properties of shape
▶ recognising/using language
▶ recognising relationships between properties
positions, directions and patterns
▶ using language of position and direction
▶ copying/describing patterns
▶ making spatial representations

independent
properties of shape
▶ explaining shape names
positions, directions and patterns
▶ making patterns with rules
▶ reading spatial representations

Find the treasure

Children find hidden 'treasure' by following a trail which begins with a line of mixed shapes then divides into several trails of just one shape, with the trail of circles leading to the treasure. When you have laid the trail, tell the children to follow the circles to find the treasure.

You will need

- *shiny plastic jewellery for 'treasure'*
- *circle, triangle and square shapes of different sizes*

> Main aims

- to promote an interest in shapes
- to develop recognition of 2D shapes

💬 Things to talk about

- the properties of the shapes: how many **sides, corners**
- the similarities and differences between the shapes
- different sizes of shapes. *Which is the biggest triangle?*

❓ Do the children...

- refer to the shapes by name?
- discuss the differences in the properties using their own words?

🤸 Further challenges

- Children follow a trail including some irregular and less common shapes, some 3D.
- The children are involved in setting up the trail.

beginner
properties of shape
▶ interest in shapes
positions, directions and patterns
▶ interest in positions, directions and patterns

apprentice
properties of shape
▶ recognising/using language
▶ recognising relationships between properties
positions, directions and patterns
▶ using language of position and direction
▶ copying/describing patterns
▶ making spatial representations

independent
properties of shape
▶ explaining shape names
positions, directions and patterns
▶ making patterns with rules
▶ reading spatial representations

Fill the shape

Children create pictures with blocks, draw round the outline and challenge others to fill in the outline with shapes, fitting the outline exactly and leaving no gaps.

You will need
- *construction materials: wooden blocks, Lego, Pattern Blocks*

> Main aims
- to experience properties of shapes
- to investigate how shapes fit together and how moving them changes the relationship between shapes

💬 Things to talk about
- *Why is this like laying carpet/tiling the bathroom/brick laying?*
- *Which shapes fit together leaving no gaps? Why?* Use **corner, straight, curved, length of sides**
- the names of shapes: **square, triangle, hexagon, circle**
- how shapes can be arranged; use positional language: **next to, on top of, underneath**

❓ Do the children...
- use appropriate mathematical language?
- identify properties of shapes and use these to help them select appropriate shapes to fill spaces, rather than trial and error?

✿ Further challenge
- Children can play a game with a shape dice which matches the 'Pattern Blocks', collecting shapes to fill their outline.

beginner
properties of shape
▶ interest in shapes
positions, directions and patterns
▶ interest in positions, directions and patterns

apprentice
properties of shape
▶ recognising/using language
▶ recognising relationships between properties
positions, directions and patterns
▶ using language of position and direction
▶ copying/describing patterns
▶ making spatial representations

independent
properties of shape
▶ explaining shape names
positions, directions and patterns
▶ making patterns with rules
▶ reading spatial representations

Roaming robot

The children direct a programmable robot, first in a straight line, then in such a way as to knock down several piles of boxes in an open space.

You will need
- *a programmable robot (such as Roamer, PIP or Pixie)*
- *cardboard boxes*
- *Post-its*

> Main aim
- to develop the language of position and directions

💬 Things to talk about
- the order of key presses the robot understands
- *What happens when the keys are pressed? Which key is pressed to make it turn left or right?*
- to reach the boxes, whether the robot needs to go **further, not so far, forwards** or **backwards, left** or **right**
- *Do you need a **bigger** or **smaller** number to knock down the boxes?*

❓ Do the children...
- use words like *forwards, backwards, left* or *right*?
- choose the correct key to go forwards or backwards?
- choose the correct key to go left or right?

✱ Further challenge
- Children can direct the robot on a route marked on the floor to reach the boxes, or to deliver letters (Post-its on the robot) to numbered box 'houses'.

beginner
properties of shape
▶ interest in shapes
positions, directions and patterns
▶ interest in positions, directions and patterns

apprentice
properties of shape
▶ recognising/using language
▶ recognising relationships between properties
positions, directions and patterns
▶ using language of position and direction
▶ copying/describing patterns
▶ making spatial representations

independent
properties of shape
▶ explaining shape names
positions, directions and patterns
▶ making patterns with rules
▶ reading spatial representations

Block caterpillar

Children build a caterpillar or other creature from blocks. Ideally this activity would follow a minibeast search.

You will need

- unit blocks or similar with a wide variety of shapes

> Main aims

to provide opportunities for children:

- to represent a real life experience in 3D materials
- to think about and discuss the similarity in shape and position between caterpillar parts and blocks

💬 Things to talk about

- *What shapes can you see on the different parts of the caterpillar?* (e.g. **circular**, **cylindrical** body shapes, **cuboid** legs)
- which shapes go next to each other, above, below, on top of, between

❓ Do the children...

- use vocabulary *like next to, above, below, on top of, between?*
- select appropriate shapes to make a 3D representation?
- select alternative shapes if certain blocks are not available?
- show how the shapes fit together to make the caterpillar without teacher intervention?

🏃 Further challenge

- Children can make other creatures from blocks.

beginner
properties of shape
▸ interest in shapes
positions, directions and patterns
▸ interest in positions, directions and patterns

apprentice
properties of shape
▸ recognising/using language
▸ recognising relationships between properties
positions, directions and patterns
▸ using language of position and direction
▸ copying/describing patterns
▸ making spatial representations

independent
properties of shape
▸ explaining shape names
positions, directions and patterns
▸ making patterns with rules
▸ reading spatial representations

Washing line game

Children continue a given pattern of two coloured 'socks' on a washing line, describing what they are doing and why. Children then start patterns for others to continue.

You will need

- *washing line*
- *selection of contrasting colour and length socks made from paper or material*
- *pegs*

> Main aims

- to develop the language of position and order
- to create, describe and predict patterns

💬 Things to talk about

- *Which socks are the same length/colour/pattern?*
- where they are in the sequence: **next to, before, after**
- the order: **first, second**
- ways of patterning

❓ Do the children...

- predict what will come next?
- describe the pattern or explain why they have continued it in a certain way?
- make up their own pattern

🏃 Further challenge

- Children continue a more difficult pattern with three items or a reversed order.

beginner
properties of shape
> interest in shapes
positions, directions and patterns
> interest in positions, directions and patterns

apprentice
properties of shape
> recognising/using language
> recognising relationships between properties
positions, directions and patterns
> using language of position and direction
> copying/describing patterns
> making spatial representations

independent
properties of shape
> explaining shape names
positions, directions and patterns
> making patterns with rules
> reading spatial representations

Building from plans

Children construct a house (room, boat or bus) on a base plan. As they build on the plan, they become increasingly selective about the size and properties of the solid shapes they use.

You will need
- *building blocks such as unit blocks*
- *plan for a building*

> Main aims
- to use spatial representations
- to investigate and use the relationships between shape properties

💬 Things to talk about
- what we use plans for, e.g. buildings
- *What will the finished model look like?*
- how we will put the blocks on the plan
- the edges of the shapes; whether they are too **long, short, narrow, wide**
- the names of shapes: **cuboid, cube.**
- *What is the same about these shapes?* (e.g. having **straight sides, square corners**)
- *Will that block still fit if you turn it a different way?*

❓ Do the children...
- talk about the properties of the shapes they need?
- use shape properties to help select from the pile, rather than use trial and error?
- try turning or rotating shapes as they fit them?
- explain how the plan relates to the possible models?

🏃 Further challenge
- Children build following photographs of models made using the construction material available, e.g. unit blocks, Lego, Quadro, Techni.

beginner
properties of shape
▶ interest in shapes
positions, directions and patterns
▶ interest in positions, directions and patterns

apprentice
properties of shape
▶ recognising/using language
▶ recognising relationships between properties
positions, directions and patterns
▶ using language of position and direction
▶ copying/describing patterns
▶ making spatial representations

independent
properties of shape
▶ explaining shape names
positions, directions and patterns
▶ making patterns with rules
▶ reading spatial representations

Kite flying

Children compare the way differently shaped kites fly. This gives them the opportunity to discuss shapes in a stimulating and purposeful context.

You will need
- *kites of different shapes, previously made by the children*

> Main aims
- promote an interest in shapes
- to discuss the properties of shapes and relate these to a purpose
- to use the language of position and movement

Things to talk about
- the similarities and differences between two differently shaped kites; use the shape names (**triangle, square, circle**), and the language of properties: **side** and **corner** for 2D; **edge** and **face** for 3D shapes
- how the kites move; use **over, under, twist and turn, in front of, behind**
- *Which kite flies **highest/lowest**?*
- how we could rate the kites from most to least successful

? Do the children...
- use appropriate language to describe position and movement?
- identify which properties of the shapes are the same and which are different?

Further challenge
- Children can compare 2D and 3D kites in terms of shape and success in flight.

beginner
properties of shape
▷ interest in shapes
positions, directions and patterns
▷ interest in positions, directions and patterns

apprentice
properties of shape
▷ recognising/using language
▷ recognising relationships between properties
positions, directions and patterns
▷ using language of position and direction
▷ copying/describing patterns
▷ making spatial representations

independent
properties of shape
▷ explaining shape names
positions, directions and patterns
▷ making patterns with rules
▷ reading spatial representations

Making a den

One way children get into spaces is by making dens. Dens can be indoors or out, so long as they are big enough for children to get inside.

You will need
- *large cardboard boxes and pieces of fabric, such as tablecloths, curtains or blankets*

> Main aims
- to give the children the opportunity to plan the use of a large space
- to develop spatial language

💬 Things to talk about
- what size and shape the den needs to be
- *How many of you will fit inside?*
- what kind of material will be needed

❓ Do the children...
- collect together the appropriate materials, showing they are visualising the shape of the finished den?
- begin by building an appropriate height or perimeter?
- discuss how to enclose the top of the den, using positional language: (*on top of, underneath*), and language of properties (*sides, corners*)?

🏃 Further challenge
- Children build a den for a given number of children to get inside.

beginner level
properties of shape
▶ interest in shapes
positions, directions and patterns
▶ interest in positions, directions and patterns

apprentice level
properties of shape
▶ recognising/using language
▶ recognising relationships between properties
positions, directions and patterns
▶ using language of position and direction
▶ copying/describing patterns
▶ making spatial representations

independent level
properties of shape
▶ explaining shape names
positions, directions and patterns
▶ making patterns with rules
▶ reading spatial representations

Bike and trike park

Organising a parking area provides opportunities for designing the use of a space. When children do this for the nursery's bikes and trikes, they are involved in fitting irregular shapes together.

You will need
- *outdoor area big enough for several ride-on toys*
- *chalk, powder paint or car parking tape*

> Main aims
- to fit irregular shapes together
- to use language of position

💬 Things to talk about
- *What happens when we park the trikes?*
- *How can we mark the spaces and make the lines straight?*
- *Which shapes will be best for the parking spaces?*
- How are vehicles parked? Use language of position and movement: **next to, alongside, in front of, behind, front, back, in** and **out, reversing, turning, left** and **right.**

❓ Do the children...
- suggest an appropriate space and arrangement?
- select vehicles of similar shape and size to go together?
- suggest routes within the car park, entrance and exit?

🏃 Further challenge
- Children draw a map of the vehicle park to be displayed at the entrance, with numbered spaces.

beginner
properties of shape
▶ interest in shapes
positions, directions and patterns
▶ interest in positions, directions and patterns

apprentice
properties of shape
▶ recognising/using language
▶ recognising relationships between properties
positions, directions and patterns
▶ using language of position and direction
▶ copying/describing patterns
▶ making spatial representations

independent
properties of shape
▶ explaining shape names
positions, directions and patterns
▶ making patterns with rules
▶ reading spatial representations

Hide and seek

Hide and seek can become an enjoyable maths game if children are encouraged to guess at hiding places and describe them.

> Main aims
- to foster an interest in positions
- to use the language of position

💬 Things to talk about
- where the children think the person is hidden; use **behind, underneath, next to, above, in front of**
- *What makes a good hiding place?*
- clues to where the child is hidden. *Is she near the bookrack/between the graphics area and the sand?*
- the boundaries for the game, i.e. how far away they can hide

? Do the children...
- respond to clues using positional words?
- describe where they found the hidden child, using such language?

🏃 Further challenge
- Children can hide objects and give clues to others.

beginner
properties of shape
▶ interest in shapes
positions, directions and patterns
▶ interest in positions, directions and patterns

apprentice
properties of shape
▶ recognising/using language
▶ recognising relationships between properties
positions, directions and patterns
▶ using language of position and direction
▶ copying/describing patterns
▶ making spatial representations

independent
properties of shape
▶ explaining shape names
positions, directions and patterns
▶ making patterns with rules
▶ reading spatial representations

Step hop

Movement and dance can help children to develop their awareness of shape and space through large motor activity. Children devise a step hop dance routine which takes them all around the edges of large foam shapes or mats. Encourage them to feel all the corners, the straight edges and curves

You will need
- *large foam shapes or mats*

> Main aims
- to physically experience and discuss properties of shapes
- to experience and discuss moving in different directions

💬 Things to talk about
- the corners and sides of the shapes, how many there are, and whether **straight** or **curved**
- *Does the dance go **along, around, left** or **right**?*
- *What is the best place to start your dance?*

❓ Do the children...
- identify the sides and corners of the shape?
- justify the starting place for their dance?
- compose a dance routine that takes them completely around the outside of their shape?
- talk about the directions they move in?

🤸 Further challenge
- Children describe walking around the nursery building and draw the route.

beginner
properties of shape
▸ interest in shapes
positions, directions and patterns
▸ interest in positions, directions and patterns

apprentice
properties of shape
▸ recognising/using language
▸ recognising relationships between properties
positions, directions and patterns
▸ using language of position and direction
▸ copying/describing patterns
▸ making spatial representations

independent
properties of shape
▸ explaining shape names
positions, directions and patterns
▸ making patterns with rules
▸ reading spatial representations

127

Routines and Special Events

TIDY-UP TIME

How long does it take?

Children can have fun and learn about time by using wind-up toys as timers. First they can play with the timers, and later perform a tidying-up task (e.g. putting the books away) while the toy ticks.

> Main aims
- to develop awareness of the passing of time
- to use the language of time
- to compare lengths of time directly

💬 Things to talk about
- starting the timer and the job at the same time
- *Do you think you can sweep up the sand before the penguin stops moving?*
- whether it will take more time or less if two children are sweeping
- *How can you tell who was the fastest?*

❓ Do the children...
- talk about how long it takes to finish an activity (*before* or *after* the penguin stops)?
- compare their activity with the timer using words such as *faster* or *slower*?

🤸 Further challenges
- Introduce other sorts of timers to time the activity.
- Sing a song as a timer (e.g. how many verses of a song to complete task).

beginner
▶showing an interest in measures
▶comparing visually

apprentice
▶using the language of measures
▶using direct comparison
▶ordering three or more things
▶engaging with measurement and tools

independent
▶using measuring units and tools

Tidying up the shapes

Children can learn a lot about shapes when tidying boxes and other packaging materials in the design and technology area. For instance, if you decide to keep the cylinders separately, children can sort cardboard tubes from boxes and other packaging. If you ask the children to fit boxes into a limited space, they will have to turn them around and fit them together in different ways.

You will need
• blocks of found materials to tidy away
• boxes, labels

Main aims
• to develop the language of properties of shape
• to explore relationships between properties of shape

Things to talk about
• *What different kinds of shapes are there? How can we use them when making constructions?* e.g. What shapes are good for wheels?
• *How might we sort them so that we can find the ones we want? How shall we label them?* (pictures or words)
• *How can we fit them best into a small space?* (biggest first? turn them round to fit in different ways?)

Do the children...
• sort the packaging materials according to shape, rather than colour or function?
• use shape language such as *round, flat, box* as well as *cylinder?*
• try different ways of fitting shapes together?

Further challenge
• The children could match a solid shape to a two-dimensional representation. The silhouettes can also be used to help children hang tools back in the right places.

beginner
properties of shape
▶ interest in shapes
positions, directions and patterns
▶ interest in positions, directions and patterns

apprentice
properties of shape
▶ recognising/using language
▶ recognising relationships between properties
positions, directions and patterns
▶ using language of position and direction
▶ copying/describing patterns
▶ making spatial representations

independent
properties of shape
▶ explaining shape names
positions, directions and patterns
▶ making patterns with rules
▶ reading spatial representations

Beat the count

To make a game of tidying up a specific area, nominate some children to count to 10. This practice of saying the number sequence can be extended to higher numbers with the support of an adult.

> Main aims
- to say number words in sequence
- to use number word patterns

⬭ Things to talk about
- *Did you finish tidying up before the count reached 10?*
- counting higher and spotting patterns of teens and twenties

? Do the children...
- recite most of the numbers to 10 confidently?
- count to 20, 30 or beyond, or use patterns they have invented, like 'eleventeen', or 'twenty-ten'?

Further challenge
- Count higher!

Pens in the pot

Labelling pots helps to check that none are lost, and demonstrates a real purpose for using numerals, linking them to numbers of things. You can also pose problems about how many are missing.

> Main aims
- to engage children's interest in and recognition of numerals
- to match numerals to amounts
- to read numerals for a purpose

💬 Things to talk about
- how we use numerals to check that we have not lost things, e.g. on boxed games or jigsaws
- how many things are missing; for instance, if there should be 6 red pens and there are only 4, how many are missing

❓ Do the children...
- talk about number names, but not always the right ones?
- recognise the numbers, but not check the amount?
- read the numerals and count to check?
- conclude how many are missing?

🔆 Further challenge
- The children can help you make the labels.

You will need
- labels to match the numbers of things that should be in the containers, e.g. 10 big crayons, 6 pairs of scissors
- examples of boxed games or jigsaws with labels numbering the contents

Tidy lists

Children who are beginning to read numerals can be given lists, supported by pictures, to help them tidy up, e.g. 4 Lego bricks.

> Main aims
- to engage children's interest in and recognition of symbols
- to match numerals to amounts

💬 Things to talk about
- how some adults have to do a lot of reading numbers and counting
- the numerals in the nursery room and what these mean

❓ Do the children...
- count the objects and stop at the required number?
- recognise the numerals but ignore them when counting?
- use the 'tidy list' numbers to put the right number of toys away?

🔆 Further challenge
- Use higher numbers; make the labels with the children.

You will need
- 'lists'–cards with pictures (cut from catalogues)

beginner
number and counting
▶comparing
▶saying number words in sequence
▶setting out by eye or 1–1 correspondence
number symbols
▶awareness of numerals

apprentice
number and counting
▶counting objects, one for one
▶using the 'last word' rule
▶counting out a specific number of objects
▶using number language
number symbols
▶using own symbols
▶interest in/recognition of numerals

independent
number and counting
▶knowing what counting is used for
▶adding and subtracting practically
▶solving number problems
number symbols
▶matching numerals with amounts
▶writing numerals
▶reading and writing for a purpose

133

CHECKING NUMBERS

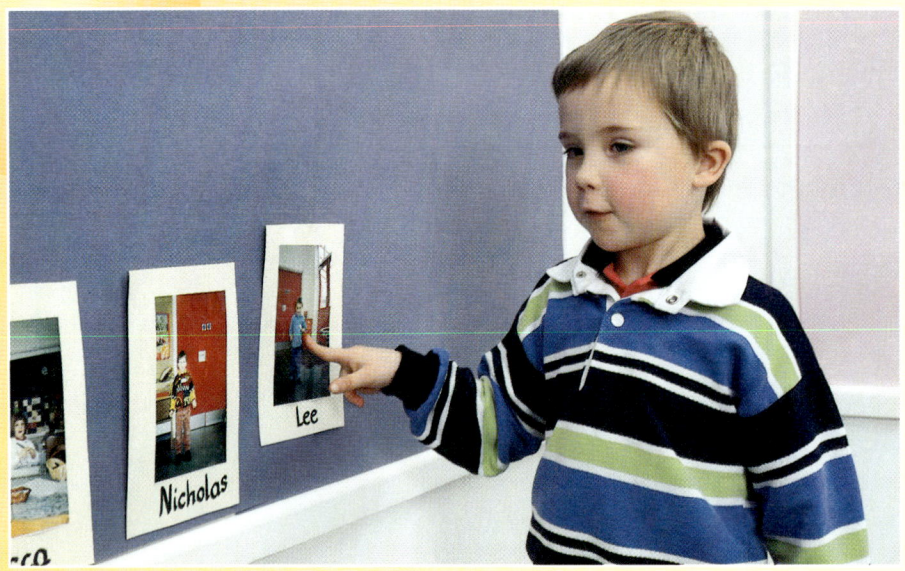

Who's here?

Children can take part in 'finding out who's here' by sticking a name card, picture or photo of themselves on a chart as they enter the nursery. This chart can then be a focus for everyday counting, with numerals to stick to the board.

> Main aims

- to join in counting for a purpose
- to record the number of children present
- to link numerals to amounts

💬 Things to talk about

- *Why do we need to know how many children are at the nursery each time?* (number of toys/drinks to set out, fire drill)
- *What can we do to show how many children are at the nursery?* (write or attach the number)
- how to take pictures off the board when we go home *Will there be* **more** *or* **not as many** *faces then?*

? Do the children...

- say the number words in sequence when counting all the pictures?
- count and say how many children are present, e.g. to hear a story, eat their lunch?
- read the numeral?

🤸 Further challenges

- Talk about who arrives (and leaves) first, second, third, fourth, etc.
- The children can select written number cards to match the total number of children present.

Are you here?

This is an everyday activity which helps children realise how adults use numbers and counting to answer the question 'How many children are here today?' Count heads out loud with the children, giving the younger ones an opportunity to join in.

You will need

- large whiteboard or Velcro board
- *an attachable symbol for each child (photo or name card)*
- *attachable numerals*

> Main aims

- to join in counting
- to count using one number word for one person
- to create contexts for children to calculate and predict

💬 Things to talk about

- *How can we find out how many children are sitting on the mat?*
- *How will we know who has been counted?*
- *Supposing more children arrive; will the total be a **smaller** or **larger** number?*
- whether a number line would be helpful

? Do the children...

- say the number words in sequence with you?
- use words like *more, many*?
- say a number word for each person they are counting?
- relate the numbers they say to the final amount?
- talk about how many children there will be 'if one more comes', 'if two more come'?

beginner
number and counting
▶comparing
▶saying number words in sequence
▶setting out by eye or 1–1 correspondence
number symbols
▶awareness of numerals

apprentice
number and counting
▶counting objects, one for one
▶using the 'last word' rule
▶counting out a specific number of objects
▶using number language
number symbols
▶using own symbols
▶interest in/recognition of numerals

independent
number and counting
▶knowing what counting is used for
▶adding and subtracting practically
▶solving number problems
number symbols
▶matching numerals with amounts
▶writing numerals
▶reading and writing for a purpose

FOOD TIMES

Drinks, fruit, snacks and meals afford ample opportunities for one-to-one matching and counting. For instance, giving one thing to each person is a way of finding out if there are enough (or too many); counting is another way of solving the same problem. If there are large numbers of small items then children can talk about whether there is enough to have two or three each. If there are pieecs of fruit, they can discuss how many smaller pieces they need to be cut into.

Biscuit time

> ### Main aims
> - to match people with objects using one-to-one correspondence
> - to count out amounts
> - to count the number of children and food items and compare them

You will need
- *fruit or snack food, plates*

💬 Things to talk about
- how we can share things out by giving one thing to each person, and how there may not be **enough** or there may be some **left over**
- *Shall we count the children round the table to see how many biscuits we need?*
- *Who will count the biscuits to see if there are **enough**?*

❓ Do the children...
- share the biscuits out giving one to each child?
- count the biscuits/children? say the last number as the whole amount, when asked?
- spontaneously use their number totals to compare people and biscuits?
- suggest how many pieces the fruit should be cut into, making reasonable estimates?

🏃 Further challenge
- Children can make a written order by drawing items of food and recording the number of children 'ordering' each item beneath.

Birthday maths

A child's birthday can be an excellent opportunity to interact for an extended time with one child, to everyone's enjoyment and benefit. Birthday maths can involve opportunities for counting, sharing out food items and thinking about being one year older. If there is a large number in the group it will involve counting to numbers over ten.

You will need
- *a child with a birthday*
- *cake with candles, cards or sweets*

Main aims
- to compare sets using one-to-one correspondence
- to count and find 'how many' using one number word per

Things to talk about
- *Whose birthday is it today? When is your birthday?*
- what we can count on a birthday (cards, candles, invitations, stamps)
- *How do we know how much food/how many sweets we need to have enough for everyone?*

Do the children...
- count candles or puffs along with the other children, without really linking this to quantity?
- count the children at each table?
- say how many pieces of birthday cake to put out?

Further challenges
- Talk about how we are one year older, one year **more** than we were last year, on our birthday. Children put one more candle to show next year's birthday, or remove a candle to show last year's.
- Children make cards with numerals for this birthday, and the next, and last year's.
- Children find the date of a birthday on a calendar.

beginner
number and counting
- comparing
- saying number words in sequence
- setting out by eye or 1–1 correspondence
number symbols
- awareness of numerals

apprentice
number and counting
- counting objects
- using the 'last word' rule
- setting out a specific number of objects
- using number language
number symbols
- using own symbols
- interest in/recognition of numerals

independent
number and counting
- knowing what counting is used for
- calculating
- solving number problems
number symbols
- matching numerals with amounts
- writing numerals
- reading and writing for a purpose

PARTIES

Parties take place in many different forms and contexts. Involving children in preparing for them gives important experience of putting mathematics to real use. Whether you are celebrating a particular festival or occasion, planning a tea party or picnic, sharing with a few or inviting all the parents, children can join in the planning decisions and preparation and then rehearse the activities involved in roleplay subsequently.

All areas of maths are involved. The following are some examples.

Voting

Children can vote on different options for food or games. For instance, you can gather suggestions for different flavours of cakes to make, then draw quick illustrations for these. Children can choose which picture to go and stand by, then record tallies and count them. Alternatively, children could draw pictures of their choice and stick these under pictures of the options. Sticking name cards and strips of Velcro under pictures is another method of recording votes. You can write numerals too.

> Aims

- to count to compare
- to give experience of recording amounts and interpreting picture graphs

💬 Things to talk about

- *What do we like best?*
- *How do we decide what to make so we don't waste anything?*
- *How could we record our votes?*
- *What do these show?*

❓ Do the children...

- count the votes and say how many there are?
- read the numerals from the chart?
- count the children and compare the numbers?
- interpret the results, e.g. *More people want...*

🏃 Further challenges

- How many different sandwiches could be made using two breads and two spreads?
- How many tables are needed for the number of people sitting in fours?

beginner
number and counting
▶comparing
▶saying number words in sequence
▶setting out by eye or 1–1 correspondence
number symbols
▶awareness of numerals

apprentice
number and counting
▶counting objects, one for one
▶using the 'last word' rule
▶counting out a specific number of objects
▶using number language
number symbols
▶using own symbols
▶interest in/recognition of numerals

independent
number and counting
▶knowing what counting is used for
▶adding and subtracting practically
▶solving number problems
number symbols
▶matching numerals with amounts
▶writing numerals
▶reading and writing for a purpose

Drinks

Children can work out how much squash they will need for the whole group. They can work out how many litre bottlefuls will be needed for the whole group, by pouring the same amount into the right number of glasses, which may be of different but the same capacity.

You will need

- *a standard-sized beaker*
- *glasses (short, wide, tall, narrow)*
- *juice, coloured water*
- *litre bottle*

> Main aims

- to develop an interest in measures
- to use appropriate language
- to give children experience of using non-standard units

💬 Things to talk about

- fairness – how we need a standard-sized beaker for everyone
- how to measure how many cupfuls from a bottle
- how to check there is enough for everyone

? Do the children...

- use appropriate language, e.g. my glass is *wide/narrow?*
- say that drinks that come from the same measure must be the same, and explain why they may <u>look</u> different?

Further challenge

- Decide on the order of events: e.g. do we eat before games?

beginner
▶ showing an interest in measures
▶ comparing visually

apprentice
▶ using the language of measures
▶ using direct comparison
▶ ordering three or more things
▶ engaging with measurement and tools

independent
▶ using measuring units and tools

Hats

Making different-shaped hats, from simple crowns to triangular and conical hats, gives children opportunities to experience the change from 2D to 3D, and discuss the effects.

Main aims
- to relate 2D to 3D shapes
- to use the language of shapes

Things to talk about
- *What shapes are best for hats?* – cones/cylinders for crowns?
- what shapes look like when 'flat' and made up, e.g. rectangles turn into cylinder crowns
- *Can we predict what the hat will look like?*
- the stages for making a hat (first decide shape, make one, adapt)
- *How can we stick it together and make it fit?*

Do the children...
- choose the right shapes to fold and fit together?
- use appropriate language, e.g. *round, pointed, rectangle, cone?*

Further challenge
- Make different-shaped placemats, decorations.

beginner
properties of shape
❯ interest in shapes
positions, directions and patterns
❯ interest in positions, directions and patterns

apprentice
properties of shape
❯ recognising/using language
❯ recognising relationships between properties
positions, directions and patterns
❯ using language of position and direction
❯ copying/describing patterns
❯ making spatial representations

independent
properties of shape
❯ explaining shape names
positions, directions and patterns
❯ making patterns with rules
❯ reading spatial representations

GOING FOR A WALK

A walk outside the nursery can be an occasion to focus on numbers in a variety of contexts and to talk about and draw maps. Some written numbers such as speed limit signs will relate to measures and there will be opportunities to talk about distance and time.

Number walk

The children can count numbers in the context of a game about *'How many did we see?'* Decide what you are going to count, such as cats and dogs, or lorries and bikes. You can help the children to record their counting with tallies and a number clicker or a calculator. Let one child be the 'recorder' and the other children be the 'counters'. Use a large calculator and program it with '+1='. Show the 'recorder' how every time the '=' button is pressed the number display goes one higher. Encourage the recorder to press the button carefully each time a child calls out 'there's one' or 'that's four' and to keep the display until the walk's over. Back in the nursery, invite the children to draw what they counted.

> ### Main aims
> - to foster an interest in counting things
> - to record counts mechanically
> - to read environmental numbers and calculator numbers

💬 Things to talk about

- counting things outside the nursery – trees, flowers, cats for instance
- how when we go on a walk there are lots of things to count and it can make a good game to see how many things there are
- how we can use a calculator or a number clicker to count for us by pressing a button each time we see something we're counting

❓ Do the children...

- join in with the game and (mostly) call out only when they see an item that's being counted? Call out *'there's one (two, three, etc.)'* but not very accurately?
- draw the number of buses, cats, etc. they saw on their walk? recognise some numbers on buses, houses etc.?
- use the calculator or number clicker to remember the total items seen?
- use the numbers to compare?

beginner
number and counting
▶ comparing
▶ saying number words in sequence
▶ setting out by eye or 1–1 correspondence
number symbols
▶ awareness of numerals

apprentice
number and counting
▶ counting objects, one for one
▶ using the 'last word' rule
▶ counting out a specific number of objects
▶ using number language
number symbols
▶ using own symbols
▶ interest in/recognition of numerals

independent
number and counting
▶ knowing what counting is used for
▶ adding and subtracting practically
▶ solving number problems
number symbols
▶ matching numerals with amounts
▶ writing numerals
▶ reading and writing for a purpose

How long will it take?

Children can alter the speed at which they walk by taking small steps or large strides, walking fast or hopping. Using a sandtimer they can see how this affects the time taken and predict whether they will be faster or slower than the timer.

You will need
- *one or more sand-timers*

▶ Main aims

- to focus on speed and the passage of time
- to use the language of time
- to experience using a timer

💬 Things to talk about

- different ways we could alter the speed of walking e.g. big strides, walking fast?
- *If we hopped would it be faster or slower?*
- how the timer works
- *Can we get to the corner before the sand-timer runs out or can we walk slowly so we take longer?*

❓ Do the children...

- use the language of time: *faster, slower, quicker, taking a shorter time, more time, longer time, before, after?*
- interpret the timer e.g. say that if you finish walking after the timer runs out you take a longer time than it?

beginner
▶ showing an interest in measures
▶ comparing visually

apprentice
▶ using the language of measures
▶ using direct comparison
▶ ordering three or more things
▶ engaging with measurement and tools

independent
▶ using measuring units and tools

Journeys

Following a walk or a story about a journey, children use construction materials to recreate the route and features on the journey, giving directions as they move playpeople along the route.

You will need
- *Lego, Duplo or blocks*
- *playpeople and vehicles*
- *model road or rail tracks*

Main aims
- to develop understanding and language of position and direction
- to represent spatial relationships through pictures and symbols

Things to talk about
- *What are maps used for?*
- *Where does the journey start and end?*
- *What do you pass on the way?* order features of the journey using ordinal counting: **first, second, last**
- positions; use **near, next to, opposite**
- directions; use **forwards, straight on, turn left, turn right, go back**

Do the children...
- use appropriate language to describe direction and position?
- sequence features of the route correctly when describing the journey?
- represent the direction of the route and position of features with some accuracy?

Further challenges
- Children can make a picture of the route to nursery school.
- Children can read an enlarged or simplified map on the walk.

beginner
properties of shape
▶ interest in shapes
positions, directions and patterns
▶ interest in positions, directions and patterns

apprentice
properties of shape
▶ recognising/using language
▶ recognising relationships between properties
positions, directions and patterns
▶ using language of position and direction
▶ copying/describing patterns
▶ making spatial representations

independent
properties of shape
▶ explaining shape names
positions, directions and patterns
▶ making patterns with rules
▶ reading spatial representations

GARDENING

Designing gardens, planting bulbs, plants and seeds and measuring growth provides lots of opportunities for adults to demonstrate using mathematics for a purpose outdoors. Packets provide information on the height things will grow to and the space they need. Children can help to measure, to solve spatial and numerical problems and gain experience of the language and measuring involved.

Planting out

Different kinds of number problems arise when gardening. You may decide to have one geranium in each of the tubs and count how many you will need. You may buy a tray of plants or bag of bulbs and share them out between beds or containers.

> Aims
- to demonstrate counting for a purpose
- to give children opportunities for solving number problems

You will need
- *watering cans*
- *plots of outside garden to plant in*
- *plants, bulbs, seed*
- *gardening equipment*

💬 Things to talk about
- *How many plants should we put in each tub?*
- *How many seeds will be in each container if we share them?*
- *How can we check they all have the same amount?*

❓ Do the children...
- share out by 'dealing' one to one?
- count and say '*how many*', '*altogether*'?
- count out the right number of seeds?
- share out then count to compare they all have the same?

beginner
number and counting
▶comparing
▶saying number words in sequence
▶setting out by eye or 1–1 correspondence
number symbols
▶awareness of numerals

apprentice
number and counting
▶counting objects, one for one
▶using the 'last word' rule
▶counting out a specific number of objects
▶using number language
number symbols
▶using own symbols
▶interest in/recognition of numerals

independent level
number and counting
▶knowing what counting is used for
▶adding and subtracting practically
▶solving number problems
number symbols
▶matching numerals with amounts
▶writing numerals
▶reading and writing for a purpose

Designing gardens

Designing gardens or just planting out a border provides opportunities for children to develop spatial awareness. Visiting local parks and gardens will provide ideas and generate discussion. Children can design their own gardens on paper or by using 3D materials like blocks in the sand.

 Main aims
- to develop spatial awareness
- to represent spatial relationships

 Things to talk about
- *What sort of things could we have in a plot?* (vegetables, flowers)
- the shape of the beds and paths and the need for edgings
- *How much space do we need to grow the plants?*
- special features like ponds, bird tables, nesting boxes and where to have these

? **Do the children...**
- make suggestions for where things go?
- use spatial language?
- draw a design which shows how things relate to each other?
- refer to a design when setting out the garden?

Further challenge
- Make indoor miniature gardens in small containers of different shapes, using compost, twigs, pebbles and seeds such as cress

beginner
properties of shape
▶ interest in shapes
positions, directions and patterns
▶ interest in positions, directions and patterns

apprentice
properties of shape
▶ recognising/using language
▶ recognising relationships between properties
positions, directions and patterns
▶ using language of position and direction
▶ copying/describing patterns
▶ making spatial representations

independent
properties of shape
▶ explaining shape names
positions, directions and patterns
▶ making patterns with rules
▶ reading spatial representations

Growing

Planting seeds and bulbs in the outdoor garden area provides lots of opportunities to encourage the understanding of measures. This may evolve over time as the plants will need to grow to be measured and will need constant watering. It could be an ongoing event over the summer term. A variation of plants and vegetables would provide different lengths to measure. Sunflower seeds are always a treat as they grow fast enough to be measured frequently.

> Aims

- to compare measures, e.g. amounts of water, sizes of pots, heights of sunflowers
- to encourage estimation of measures
- to develop the language of comparison of measures
- to develop early concepts of time
- to use non-standard measures, e.g. watering cans, sticks
- to use standard measures where appropriate, e.g. centicubes, metre sticks

Things to talk about

- *How long will it take for the plants to grow and how often do they need to be checked?*
- using a calendar to record planting and check growth
- the need to water plants using the watering can – how much water do the plants need?
- how to measure the plants when they grow, e.g. marking on sticks, using Multilink, metre rules

? Do the children...

- estimate timings and lengths?
- compare the heights of plants?
- use the language of measurement, e.g. *holds more/less, longer than/shorter than, cansful, higher than?*
- talk about the records of growth and what they show?
- make the tower of centicubes the same as the plant?
- mark the height of the plant on the stick?

beginner
- showing an interest in measures
- comparing visually

apprentice
- using the language of measures
- using direct comparison
- ordering three or more things
- engaging with measurement and tools

independent
- using measuring units and tools

147

At home

Activities for parents and children

Children are exposed to mathematical ideas from their earliest years, during everyday activities, in their homes and outdoors. Young children and the adults who care for them have to deal in a practical way with mathematical problems. This gives them the opportunity to explore mathematical ideas together: working out how to fit the toys back in the box; whether there are enough biscuits for everyone; discovering what happens when a large jug of water is emptied into a small cup; talking about how long the bus will take, and whether there will be time to go to the swings.

Parents are keen to help their children at home, although they may have little time and many other pressures. They are in the unique position of being able to build on their child's interests and to adapt activities to the child's level, including involving older siblings. Sometimes parents – almost without realising they are doing it – give children a great deal of stimulus and support to make the most of these mathematical ideas. Consequently they may want to offer the teacher valuable observations of their child's responses.

But sometimes parents feel they are unable to give their children as much support as they would like, either because they do not always recognise events which are rich in mathematical potential, or because they do not know how to make the most of them. Parents also sometimes feel that they do not really understand what their child's school does to help children learn about, and understand, mathematics – especially in the early years.

In order to build on children's home experiences there needs to be a true dialogue and partnership between home and school. Children frequently demonstrate mathematical abilities at home which they do not reveal at school, perhaps for some time. When talking to parents about children's general interests, and perhaps their literacy experiences, it is easy to include some questions about mathematics. This will then enable you, for instance, to provide mathematical activities, knowing that certain children will find them familiar. For instance, you can ask children to explain to others how to play 'Snakes and Ladders' if you know they have done this a lot at home; or provide activities to extend this knowledge; or provide experiences in other mathematical areas.

In order to have a focus to your dialogue you may wish to use the following starting points:

is their child interested in:

- building with or making patterns with blocks?

- playing games which involve throwing dice, cards or turn taking

- discussing numbers which relate to them personally, such as birthday cards, door, or phone numbers

- discussing numbers around generally e.g. on buses, cars or in books

- counting: stairs, toys, fingers and toes

The following pages contain suggestions for children and parents to spend a little time together in mathematical activities. This may be doing everyday things and making the most of the mathematics involved, or playing simple games which only take a few minutes and require no special equipment. There is a great advantage in starting with these materials and then gradually making more. As children and parents begin sharing with you the things they do in maths at home you will be able to incorporate these in new games or activities.

Doubles and triples

For 2–4 players

You will need

- the number cards from a pack of playing cards

Spread all the number cards face down. Take turns to pick up three cards. If two cards are the same number you can keep both and put the other card back. If all three cards are different numbers, put them all back. The winner is the first person to find three cards with the same number, or a card with a number that matches the double already collected.

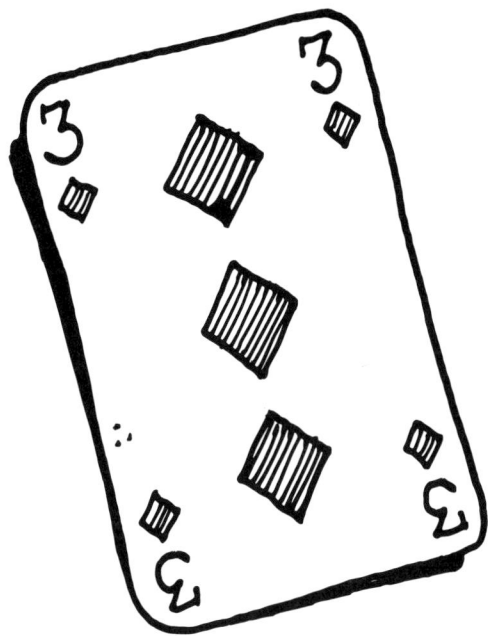

This game helps your child to identify and match numbers

151

Trains

For 2 players

You will need

- a dice
- some raisins

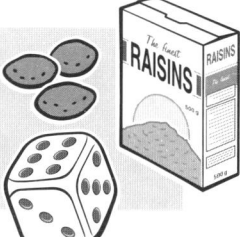

Take it in turns to throw the dice and put that number of raisins onto the train. Keep going until the carriages are full.

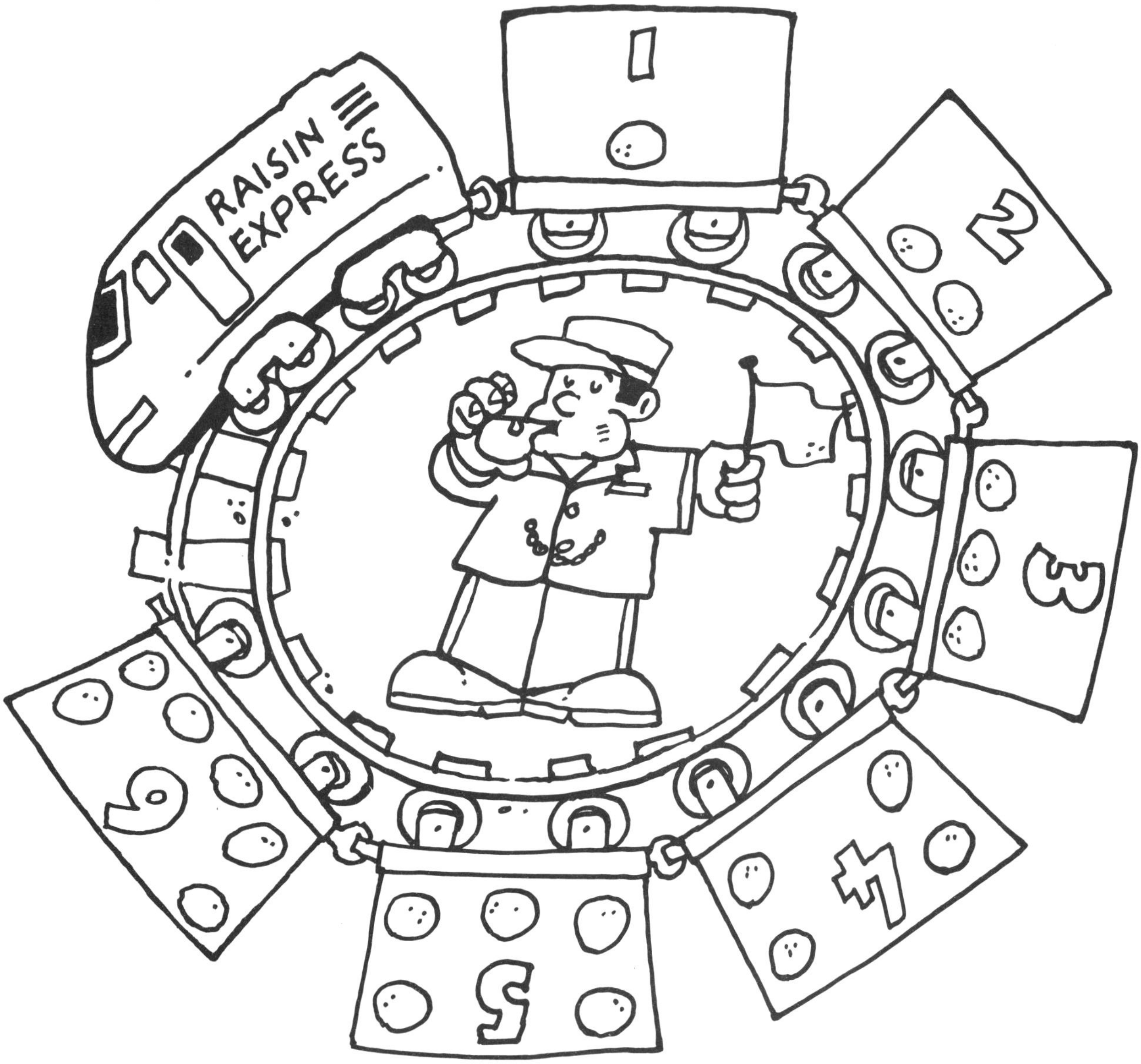

This game helps your child to count things out and recognise numbers written down

Cornflake counting

You will need

- 3 coins
- some cornflakes

For 2 players

Choose a line each and put a cornflake on each section. Then take it in turns to toss the three coins together. If there are two heads eat a cornflake from your line. If there are two tails eat a cornflake from the other line. See which cornflake line gets eaten first.

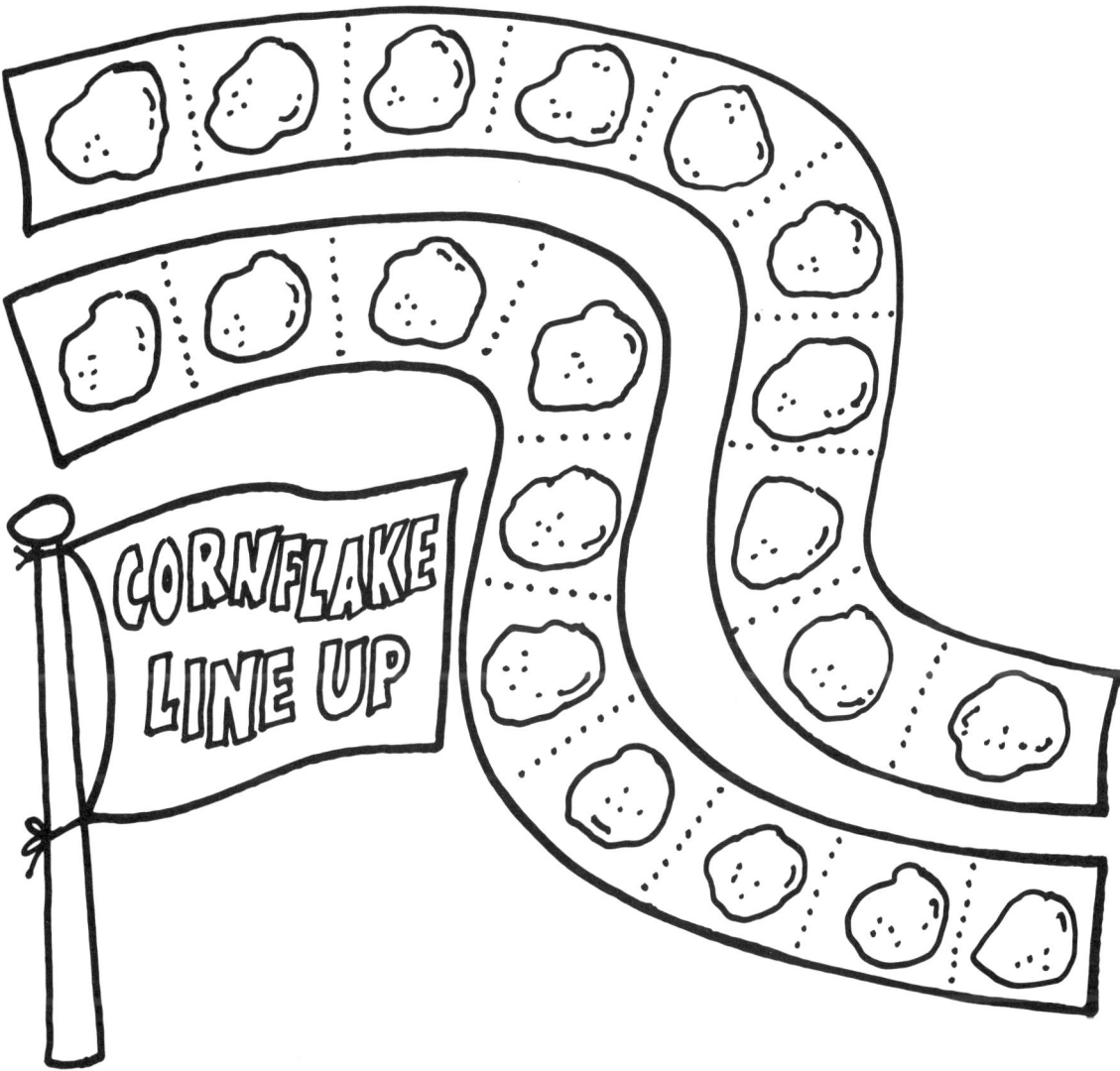

CORNFLAKE LINE UP

When your child plays this game they will do lots of counting, especially if you ask, 'How many cornflakes are left now?'

Together

For 2 players

You will need

- 2 dice
- 10–20 pennies in a pile

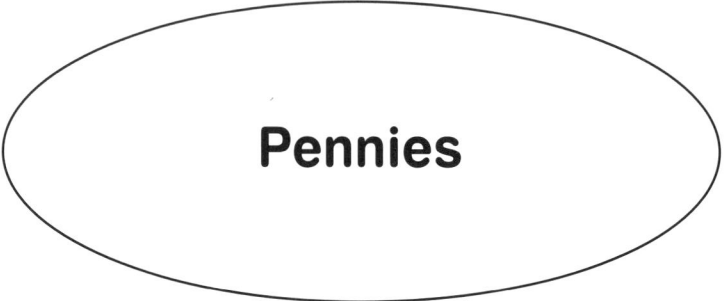

Take it in turns to throw both dice and collect that number of pennies from the pile. If the dice add up to 5 you can put them on the money box. If not, put them back in the pile. Keep taking turns until you have filled the boxes.

Pennies

When your child plays this game they are learning about addition.

Going to the bank

For 2-4 players

You will need
- a dice
- 20–40 1p coins
- 2 small cars or counters

Find 1p

Find 1p

Lose 1p | Lose 1p

Lose 1p

Find 1p

Give ten 1p coins to each player and put some extra pennies on the money pot. Take it in turns to throw the dice and count along from the house to the bank.
If you land on a Find or a Lose square you must give or take a penny from the money pot.

How many pennies do you have when you get to the Bank?

Find 1p

Lose 1p

Find 1p

Lose 1p

This game helps your child to know more about adding and taking away.

Under my hand

You will need

• 5 pennies

For 2 players

Put five pennies in the box then take it in turns to put your hand on the picture and hide some of the pennies underneath your hand. The other person has to look at the penny box and then guess how many are underneath the hand.

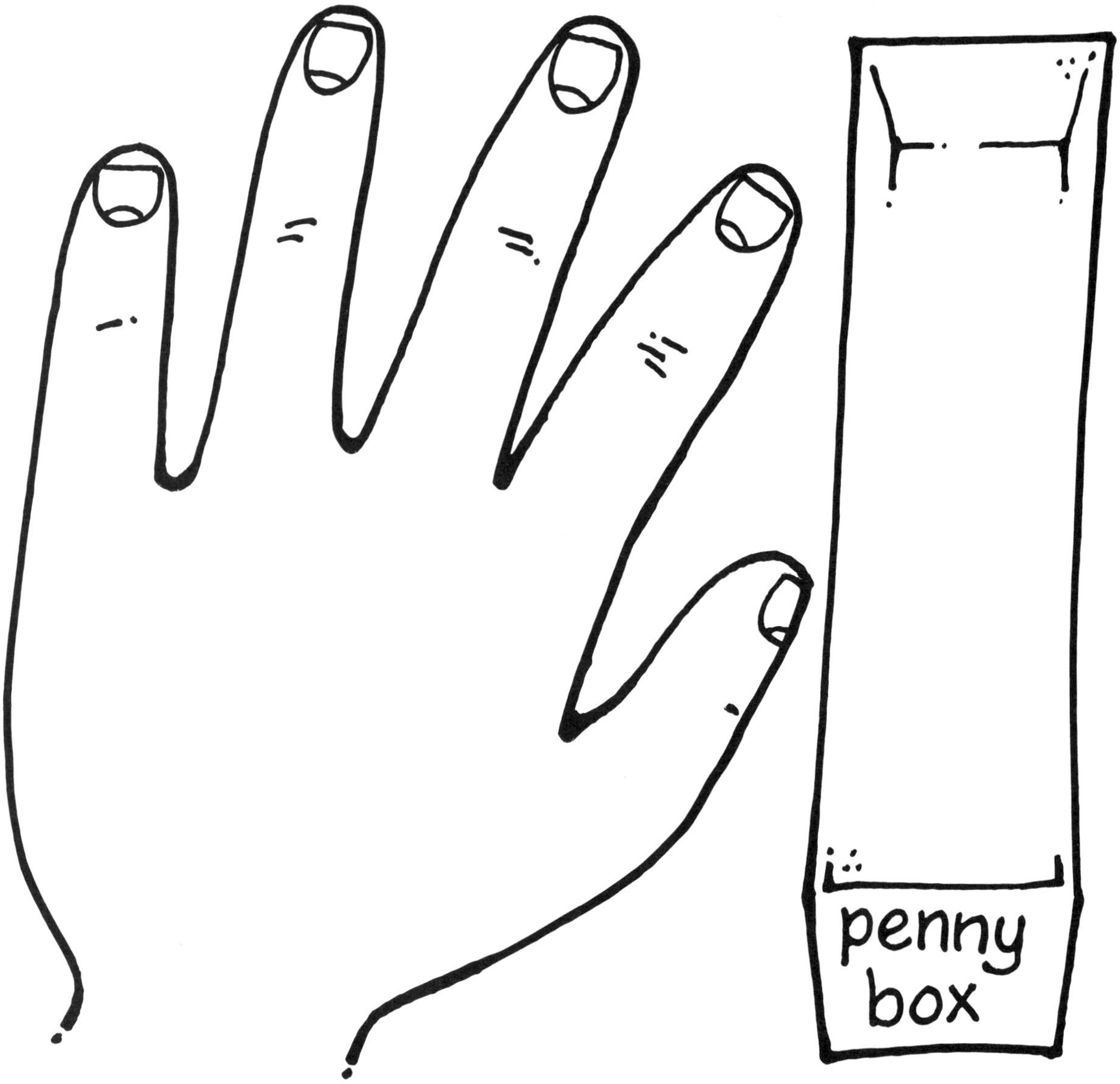

penny box

This game helps your child to develop ways of working things out in their heads.

Caterpillar count

You will need

- a dice
- some felt-tip pens or crayons

For 2–3 players

Take it in turns to throw the dice and colour in one of the caterpillar numbers. Have ten throws each and see how many caterpillars are fully coloured.

This game helps your child to count and recognise written numbers.

Three in a line

You will need

• Ace to five from each suit of a pack of playing cards

For 2–4 players

In this game you have to collect three number cards in order, such as 2, 3, 4. The colour and suit don't matter .

Shuffle the cards very well and give three cards to each person to look at. Put the rest of the shuffled cards face down on the spare card box. Then keep taking turns to take a card from the spare card box to put with your three-card collection until someone has collected three numbers in order.

This game helps your child to put numbers in order.

Ideas for rainy days

How many things can you put in a small saucepan?

Put a collection of 5 red things in a bag. What about 5 blue things, 5 green things...?

How many things can you put in the largest shoe you can find?

Use newspaper to wrap things up in parcels. Can you make a pretend parcel for everyone in your family?

Cut out paper footprints and make a trail from the front door to the kitchen.

Where else could your footprints lead to?

Ideas for out and about

On your way to the shops...

how many cats can you count? Next time you could count dogs or pigeons, bicycles, or dustbins.

As you walk along your street...

See how often you can find the number 2:

on a door   a car   a roadsign

Maybe the next day you could look for a number three.

How many steps, how many stairs up to the next floor? Can you count them in twos? How many steps between lamp–posts? What number can you see on a letter box? Do you know any telephone numbers?

160